# SOCIOLOGY

# THE BEHAVIORAL AND SOCIAL SCIENCES SURVEY
## Sociology Panel

Neil J. Smelser, *Chairman*
*University of California, Berkeley*

James A. Davis, *Co-Chairman*
*Dartmouth College*

Hubert M. Blalock
*University of North Carolina*

Otis Dudley Duncan
*University of Michigan*

Seymour Martin Lipset
*Harvard University*

Lloyd E. Ohlin
*Harvard Law School*

Ralph H. Turner
*University of California, Los Angeles*

Stanley H. Udy, Jr.
*Yale University*

# SOCIOLOGY

Edited by
Neil J. Smelser and James A. Davis

A SPECTRUM BOOK

Prentice-Hall, Inc., *Englewood Cliffs, N.J.*

Current printing (last number):
10 9 8 7 6 5 4 3 2 1

Prentice-Hall International, Inc. (*London*)
Prentice-Hall of Australia, Pty. Ltd. (*Sydney*)
Prentice-Hall of Canada, Ltd. (*Toronto*)
Prentice-Hall of India Private Limited (*New Delhi*)
Prentice-Hall of Japan, Inc. (*Tokyo*)

# FOREWORD

This book is one of a series prepared in connection with the Survey of the Behavioral and Social Sciences conducted between 1967 and 1969 under the auspices of the Committee on Science and Public Policy of the National Academy of Sciences and the Problems and Policy Committee of the Social Science Research Council.

The Survey provides a comprehensive review and appraisal of these rapidly expanding fields of knowledge, and constitutes a basis for an informed, effective national policy to strengthen and develop these fields even further.

The reports in the Survey, each the work of a panel of scholars, include studies of anthropology, economics, geography, history as a social science, political science, psychology, psychiatry as a behavioral science, sociology, and the social science aspects of statistics, mathematics and computation. A general volume discusses relations among the disciplines, broad questions of utilization of the social sciences by society, and makes specific recommendations for public and university policy.

While close communication among all concerned has been the rule, the individual panel reports are the responsibility of the panels producing them. They have not been formally reviewed or approved by the Central Planning Committee or by the sponsoring organizations. They were reviewed at an earlier stage by representatives of the National Academy of Sciences and the Social Science Research Council.

Much of the data on the behavioral and social sciences in universities used in these reports comes from a 1968 questionnaire survey, conducted by the Survey Committee, of universities offering the PhD in one of these fields. Questionnaires were filled out by PhD-granting departments (referred to as the Departmental Questionnaire); by selected professional schools (referred to as the Professional School Questionnaire); by computation centers (referred to as the Computation Center Questionnaire); by university financial offices (referred to as the Administration Questionnaire); and by research institutes, centers, laboratories and museums engaged in research in the behavioral and social sciences (referred to as the Institute Questionnaire). Further information concerning this questionnaire survey is provided in the appendix to the general report of the Central Planning Committee, *The Behavioral and Social Sciences: Outlook and Needs.*

Also included in the appendix of the report of Central Planning Committee is a discussion of the method of degree projection used in these reports, as well as some alternative methods.

### The Behavioral and Social Sciences Survey Committee
### Central Planning Committee

Ernest R. Hilgard, *Stanford University,* CHAIRMAN
Henry W. Riecken, *Social Science Research Council,*
    CO-CHAIRMAN
Kenneth E. Clark, *University of Rochester*
James A. Davis, *Dartmouth College*
Fred R. Eggan, *The University of Chicago*
Heinz Eulau, *Stanford University*
Charles A. Ferguson, *Stanford University*
John L. Fischer, *Tulane University of Louisiana*
David A. Hamburg, *Stanford University*
Carl Kaysen, *Institute for Advanced Study*
William H. Kruskal, *The University of Chicago*
David S. Landes, *Harvard University*
James G. March, *University of California, Irvine*
George A. Miller, *The Rockefeller University*
Carl Pfaffmann, *The Rockefeller University*
Neil J. Smelser, *University of California, Berkeley*
Allan H. Smith, *Washington State University*
Robert M. Solow, *Massachusetts Institute of Technology*
Edward Taaffe, *The Ohio State University*
Charles Tilly, *The University of Michigan*
Stephen Viederman, *National Academy of Sciences,* EXECUTIVE
    OFFICER

# CONTENTS

Foreword                                                              v
Preface                                                               1

**1  The Scope of Sociology**                                         5

The Questions Sociologists Ask                                        6
Sociologists at Work                                                  8
    A Field Experiment on Family Planning         8
    Studying Crime by Studying its Victims        10
    A Study of Alienation Among Workers           13
    A Survey of Intolerance                       15
    A Study of the Spread of a Wonder Drug        17
    A Pioneer Investigation of Marihuana Users    20
    A Study of Group Membership in Disaster Situations  22
    Comparative Study of Occupational Prestige    24
    Comparative Study of Changes in the Family    27
The Framework of Sociology                                            30
    Sociological Perspectives                     30
    Sociological Explanation                      32
    Sociological Theories                         33

**2  Developing Areas of Sociology**                                  37

Research Methods in Sociology: Trends and Needs                       38
    The Variety of Research Methods               38
    Unresolved Problems and Needs                 40
Comparative Study of Societies                                        43
    Traditions of Research                        43

Problems and Needs                                              46
Demography                                                      47
    The Field and Its Growth                                    47
    Historical Trends                                           49
    Current Trends and Future Needs                             54
Social Stratification                                           56
    Theoretical Analysis                                        57
    Empirical Research                                          58
    The Future of Research on Stratification                    59
Complex Organizations                                           61
    Major Approaches to the Study of Organizations              61
    Needs for Theory and Research                               64
Socialization                                                   67
    Research Trends                                             67
    Problems and Needs                                          69
Deviance and Social Control                                     72
    The Offender                                                74
    The Victim                                                  75
    The System of Social Control                                76
    The Norms That Are Violated                                 77
    The Norms of Deviant Groups                                 77
    Opportunities for Deviance                                  77
    Theory of Deviant Behavior                                  78
Social Change                                                   78
    Collective Behavior                                         79
    Modernization                                               81
    Historical Sociology                                        84
Political Sociology                                             85
    The Field and Its Focus                                     85
    Lines of Research Interest                                  86
Sociology of Education                                          90
    Education as a Sociological Variable                        90
    Schools and School Systems                                  92
    Educational Occupations                                     93
Medical Sociology                                               94
    The Definition and Patterning of Illness Behavior in
        Society                                                 95
    The Epidemiology of Disease and Impairment                  96
    Personal and Societal Response to Illness                   97
    Medical Care in the Society and the Community               98
    The Internal Organization of Medical Facilities             99
    The Relationship Between Professional and Patient           100
Obstacles to the Development of Sociological Knowledge: Some
    Speculations About Religion and Race                        101

**3 The Development of Sociology as an Academic Discipline**    **108**

Early Growth    108
Recent Trends    110

**4 Sociology and its Applications**    **116**

The Practical Importance of Sociology    116
Contributions to Policy    118
     Points of Tension and Conflict    122

**5 Manpower and Resources in Sociology**    **127**

How Many Sociologists?    128
Where Do Sociologists Work?    129
Education in Sociology Prior to Graduate Training    132
Graduate Training in Sociology    136
     Length of Time to Complete the Doctorate    138
     Quality of Training    141
     Style of Training    142
The Impending Manpower Shortage in Sociology    142
Financial Support for Sociology    146
     Federal Research Support    146
     Support and the Profession    151
Concluding Remarks    154

**6 Recommendations**    **156**

Strengthening Undergraduate Education    156
Strengthening Graduate Education    159
Strengthening Sociological Knowledge    163
Sociology and the Federal Government    168

**Appendix**    **171**

Contributors of Memoranda to the Sociology Panel on the Status
of Various Fields in the Discipline    171
Sociology Departments Participating in the Questionnaire Survey    173
Rural Sociology Departments Participating in the Questionnaire
     Survey    175

**Bibliographical Note**    **177**

CONTENTS

3 On Part Design of Scheduling and Analysis Discipline   202

    Renee C Doty
    David I Reich

4 Roadmap and its Application   218

    11 Health Services ...
    ...

5 Future and Assurance in ...

    ...

# SOCIOLOGY

# PREFACE

In 1966 the Behavioral and Social Sciences Survey Committee was appointed jointly by the National Academy of Sciences and the Social Science Research Council to report on the present status and future needs of the several behavioral and social sciences. The Survey Committee is submitting the results of its work in the form of a general report (*The Behavioral and Social Sciences: Outlook and Needs*) and special reports for each of ten disciplines. The following report by the Sociology Panel should be considered supplemental to the general report, and parallel to the panel reports for anthropology, economics, geography, history, political science, psychiatry, psychology, and statistics-mathematics-computation.

In this report we survey the discipline of sociology from several angles. First, we sample selectively the concrete things sociologists do in their research. We watch sociologists at work on an array of topics, such as worker alienation, drug usage, family life, and occupational prestige. In this sample we also include a variety of research techniques.

Second, we encompass these diverse activities in a more abstract framework that gives intellectual focus to the discipline. We outline the aspects of social life that interest sociologists, and sketch the essentials of explanation and theory in sociology.

Third, we attempt to assess the strengths, weaknesses, and future prospects of about a dozen fields, such as social stratification, political sociology, and medical sociology. Some of these fields have a long his-

1

tory of steady growth; others have shown vitality only recently; and still others must be regarded as underdeveloped. In part the survey of fields is intended to inform the reader about the status of the discipline; in part it is intended to pave the way for the specific recommendations at the end of the report.

Fourth, we survey two of the discipline's contexts. Viewing the field in historical context, we trace its early growth in American universities, and its subsequent spread to most of the rest of the world. We conclude that among the conditions that help it flourish are an open university system, a political atmosphere that protects the independence of scholars and teachers, and public recognition that sociology is relevant to social problems. Regarding the field in the context of public policy, we explore the ways that sociology can contribute to policies and decisions, and enumerate several tensions that may arise when sociologists and policy-makers meet.

Fifth, we survey the status of some of the discipline's institutional resources—especially manpower and financial support—now and in the future. We identify some problems that sociology shares with almost all the behavioral and social sciences, and we specify some that face sociology especially.

In each of these surveys we attempt to diagnose sociology's weaknesses as well as its strengths, its problems as well as its promises. We conclude the report with a number of recommendations designed to strengthen the discipline—to strengthen undergraduate and graduate education, build sociological knowledge, and improve and consolidate the relations between the profession and the federal government.

The main audience to which we direct our report includes legislators and their staffs, and decision-makers in governmental and private funding agencies. Our main objective is to indicate to this audience what sociology is about, and to convey to them our ideas about sociology's needs. A second audience is the general public; public interest in sociology is certainly growing, and we hope to supplement this interest with a modest increase in public knowledge and appreciation of the discipline. A third audience consists of our own professional colleagues and students, whose work we are attempting to present. We do not pretend to "represent" the discipline as official spokesmen; indeed, we expect some of our colleagues and students to disagree with many of our general emphases and particular statements. But we have attempted to present as realistic and balanced an account of the discipline as possible.

The work of the sociology panel began late in 1966 under the chairmanship of William H. Sewell and the co-chairmanship of Otis Dudley Duncan. At two meetings in January and February, 1967, the panel agreed upon a general outline for the report and drew up a list of several dozen knowledgeable sociologists from which we requested memoranda on the status, trends, probable future developments, and needs of their special fields of interest. The spring and summer of 1967 were devoted to commissioning and writing these memoranda. A list of those who responded to our request is appended to the report.

In the summer of 1967, Sewell resigned from the panel to assume the Chancellorship of the University of Wisconsin, Madison, and Duncan resigned as co-chairman but remained on the panel. Neil J. Smelser and James A. Davis agreed to serve as chairman and co-chairman, respectively, and in September, 1968, the four met in Berkeley to arrange the transition. At this time Ralph H. Turner and Stanley H. Udy, Jr., were added to the panel.

In October, 1967, drafting assignments were made to panel members, in accordance with their special interests and abilities. These drafts were circulated and, at a meeting in May, 1968, they were subjected to an extensive critical review. After this meeting the chairman undertook to draft a new version of the entire report, which was subjected to still further critical review by the panel at its final meeting in September, 1968.

During the drafting stage the chairman consulted a number of professional colleagues to gain their critical reactions to selected portions of the report: Howard S. Becker, Northwestern University; Robert N. Bellah, University of California, Berkeley; Reinhard Bendix, University of California, Berkeley; Robert Blauner, University of California, Berkeley; John Clausen, University of California, Berkeley; William J. Goode, Columbia University; Lewis M. Killian, University of Connecticut; and Harold L. Wilensky, University of California, Berkeley.

In the final stages of preparing the report a number of individuals offered comments and criticisms, many of which proved very helpful. We express our appreciation to the Review Panel that met in January,

1969—consisting of Peter Caws, Hunter College of the City University of New York; James S. Coleman, Johns Hopkins University; Paul Doty, Harvard University; and Albert J. Reiss, Jr., University of Michigan; and to Ernest R. Hilgard, Henry W. Riecken, Stephen Viederman, and Carl P. Swenson, Behavioral and Social Sciences Survey; Albert Biderman and Laure M. Sharp, of the Bureau of Social Science Research; Abbott L. Ferriss, Russell Sage Foundation; Howard H. Hines and Charles R. Wright, National Science Foundation; William Kruskal, University of Chicago; Eli A. Rubinstein and Kenneth G. Lutterman, National Institute of Mental Health; Elbridge Sibley, Social Science Research Council; and Nathaniel Siegel, Queens College of the City University of New York.

Special thanks are due to Mrs. Betty Lou Bradshaw and Mrs. Lucy Sells, who served as research assistants to the panel chairman, and to the staff of the Institute of Industrial Relations, University of California, Berkeley, who typed and processed the several drafts of the report.

# 1
# THE SCOPE OF
# SOCIOLOGY

To some people the word "sociology" means investigators going around and asking people personal questions; to others it means family counseling; to others it means urban renewal; to others it means doing social work with underprivileged people; to others it smacks of radical politics; and to still others it is numbers and statistics about social life.

In part, this diversity of meanings arises from the fact that sociology is a very heterogeneous enterprise. Sociologists study an extraordinary variety of topics, and it is difficult to gather all their interests into a single, convenient definition that would immediately convey the essence of the field. Another part of the diversity of meaning stems from the fact that sociologists often study things that excite strong positive or negative feelings—race relations, crime, family relations, and the like. Because of this, there is a tendency for some persons to pick out one aspect of sociology about which they feel strongly and to identify this aspect with the whole of the discipline.

Since this problem of meaning is so pronounced, we feel that our first task in this survey is to say what sociology is about. We shall take up this task in three stages. First, we shall indicate briefly what kinds of questions sociologists ask about the world. Second, we shall present a number of detailed vignettes of sociologists at work. Third, we shall sketch a more abstract view of the conceptual framework of sociology.

**5**

## THE QUESTIONS SOCIOLOGISTS ASK

Defined most generally, the mission of sociology is the scientific study of all that is social in the human condition. Sociology owes its existence to the basic fact that men and women universally organize themselves into social forms—into institutions and societies; and that their lives are, in turn, greatly influenced by these social forms. From this interest in social life flow a number of general questions:

Why and how do people go about establishing social forms?

How do people interact in social forms? What are the patterns of cooperation, competition, and conflict?

How do social forms crystallize into organizations and institutions?

How does membership in a social unit influence people's outlooks and behavior?

How do we account for the similarities and differences among social forms?

How do social forms affect one another?

Why and in what ways do social forms originate, develop, stagnate, and degenerate?

As these questions suggest, sociology has a broadly encompassing mission, because the social dimension is so omnipresent in human life. Since it considers the whole social scene, moreover, sociology is a more general discipline than some others—for example, economics, which focuses on a particular aspect of social interaction.

However general their orientation, sociologists must narrow down to very specific concerns as they attempt to increase their knowledge of social life. In the sociological study of the family, for instance, sociologists address themselves to questions like the following:

What are the family's general functions in society? Here sociologists have stressed functions like the regulation of sexual behavior and reproduction; the care of society's helpless, both young and old; the transmis-

sion of values and knowledge to new generations; and the control and transmission of property.

In what ways and why do family systems differ in the ways they perform these functions? For example, why are agriculturally based family systems locked into complex and intimate networks of grandparents, uncles and aunts, and cousins, whereas urban-industrial family systems seem more isolated from these kinsmen?

In what ways are families formed? Why do some societies have arranged marriages, while others permit free choice? In societies with voluntary marriage systems, what determines who chooses whom for a spouse—residential propinquity, common religious background, common social class background, personal compatibility, or some combination of these?

Why are some families larger than others? What is the role of social class, religion, and ethnic membership in determining patterns of fertility and size of family?

Why are some families more stable than others? Why do some social groups have higher divorce rates than others? How does prosperity and depression affect the divorce rate? What are the effects of broken families on family members?

What determines the pattern of interaction within families? Why are men typically assigned certain tasks in the family, women others? Do women who work outside the home have more influence in family decision-making than those who don't? Why do some societies experience severe conflict between adolescents and adults, while others seem to be relatively free from intergenerational conflict?

Similar lists of questions could be catalogued for the many fields in the discipline—sociology of religion, stratification, medicine, leisure, law, deviance, collective behavior, and so on. Rather than pursue this strategy, we feel that it would be more instructive to show in some detail how sociologists try to discover answers to such questions. To this end we present a number of vignettes of sociologists at work. In reading these the reader will observe a great diversity in subjects studied, questions posed, and research methods employed. Beneath this diversity, however, lies the sociologist's general preoccupation with organized social life and its impact on human behavior.

## SOCIOLOGISTS AT WORK

### A Field Experiment on Family Planning

What is the impact of educational programs that encourage family planning?

A number of social scientists from the University of Michigan, working with a community action program in Taichung, Taiwan, in 1962–63 designed an extensive and elaborate experiment to throw light on this question. Provincial health authorities in that city were launching a program to encourage families to accept family-planning services, and were making use of several educational techniques in the campaign. The job of the social scientists, who were associated with population research units based in Taiwan and at the University of Michigan, was to assess the relative impact of the several techniques.

Four different kinds of treatment were applied probabilistically to some 2,400 small neighborhoods in the city:

Method 1: Placing posters on family planning in the neighborhood and meeting with neighborhood leaders.

Method 2: Posters and meeting with leaders *plus* a direct-mail campaign.

Method 3: Posters, meeting with leaders, direct-mail campaign, *plus* personal visits with wives.

Method 4: Posters, meeting with leaders, direct-mail campaign, visits with wives, *plus* personal visits with husbands.

In addition, all the neighborhoods in the city were assigned to one of three sectors to which the four methods were applied in varying density. In the "heavy" sector half the neighborhoods, randomly selected, received intensive treatment—either Method 3 or Method 4; in the "medium" sector one third of the neighborhoods received this treatment; and in the "light" sector only one fifth.

The social scientists measured family attitudes and practices in each neighborhood *before* the educational campaign and measured them again *after* it began. Figure 1-1 shows the percentages of couples who began accepting family-planning services within the first ten months of the program, according to type and density of treatment.

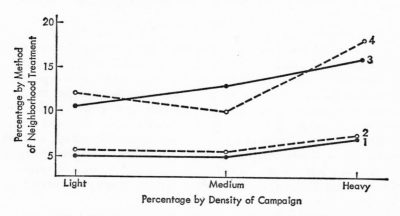

**FIGURE 1-1   PERCENTAGE OF COUPLES ACCEPTING FAMILY PLANNING SERVICES**

Source:   Drawn from data in Bernard Berelson and Ronald Freedman, "A Study in Fertility Control," *Scientific American*, 210 (May, 1964), 29–37.

As expected, both intensity and density influenced the proportion of families accepting services. The table shows that the more methods used, the greater the proportion of couples responding to the program. Moreover, the neighborhoods with more intensive treatment in the "heavy-density" sector apparently spilled over and influenced the neighborhoods with less intensive treatment in that sector. In fact, many of the acceptances were accounted for by couples who did not themselves receive home visits. Apparently some couples who were visited influenced those who were not. This suggests that such a program can have an important impact without having to saturate the entire target population with visits.

The results of the experiment also suggest that the optimum level of effort is not necessarily the highest level. It appears that the cost of visiting wives (Method 3) was well justified, because this markedly increased the proportion of acceptances over Methods 1 and 2. But the additional cost of visiting husbands as well (Method 4) produced only a negligible increase in acceptances. It is also apparent that a very respectable impact can be achieved with a density level below that used in the "heavy" sector.

This prototypical field experiment reveals that a great deal of helpful information for planners of social change can be yielded by research that incorporates many essential features of experimental design. Of course, such research does have its limitations. In most cases it is not possible in a natural setting to impose experimental controls based on random numbers as adequate controls in a laboratory setting with artificially created small groups. Moreover, both planning authorities and social scientists must be sensitive to the many ethical issues involved in social experimentation. Notwithstanding these limitations, it is often possible —and almost always helpful to both sociologist and planner—to approximate some experimental controls when new programs are initiated by planning agencies.

### Studying Crime by Studying its Victims

What is the true rate of crime in American society today? The question is of enormous importance. To answer it correctly is a necessary prelude to our understanding of criminal activity, as well as our efforts to control it. To answer it incorrectly, however, may be very damaging socially. When a police department in a given community reports a rapid increase in crime, this increase may simply reflect changes in law-enforcement practices or the increased willingness of citizens to report crime. Such reports of increased crime, therefore, may not reflect a change in the actual rate of crime in the community. This can seriously undermine public trust in the established community order and sharply curtail community activity.

As matters now stand, we have no truly reliable measures of criminal activity. Most of our knowledge rests on reports of offenses to police and on police arrests. Such statistics fall short as valid indicators on many counts. For example, they do not include crimes that are undetected, such as consumer fraud. They do not include those citizen complaints that are referred to other agencies by police departments. Furthermore, since many crimes are unsolved, police arrests of suspects are not good indicators of criminal activity. In crimes such as homicide and forcible rape, most complaints were cleared by the apprehension of suspects, but the clearance rates are as low as 23 percent for burglary and 25 percent for auto theft. Clearly, then, the official figures conceal a reservoir of undetected, unreported, and unrecorded crime.

With these problems in mind, the President's Commission on Law Enforcement and Administration came upon a new idea: to measure crime rates by asking people if they had ever been victims of crime. In 1966 the Commission sponsored a national survey of 10,000 households by the National Opinion Research Center of the University of Chicago and more intensive studies of high crime precincts in selected cities by the Bureau of Social Science Research in Washington, D.C. and the Survey Research Center of the University of Michigan.

The results were telling. The national survey showed more than twice as much criminal victimization as reported on the Index of Offenses in the Uniform Crime Reports of the FBI. Forcible rapes were more than three and one-half times the official rates, and burglaries three times. The high-crime districts in Washington, D.C., Chicago, and Boston revealed from three to ten times more offenses than were reported in the police statistics. The survey figures suggest that in high-crime districts, between 10,000 and 24,000 offenses per 100,000 persons are committed against individual residents in one year. This figure is roughly four times as great as police figures would suggest.

Though these estimates indicate a great hidden reservoir of crime, they, too, must be considered as only approximations. For several reasons they should be regarded as lower than the true rate. For example, they do not include crimes against businesses and other organizations. The survey probably also underestimates the victimization of children, since a household member proved to be more accurate in reporting offenses in which he was the victim than in reporting crimes against other members of his household. In addition, people had trouble re-calling even very serious offenses unless they had occurred recently, and minor ones were probably forgotten altogether. On the other hand, people might report to an interviewer offenses that might be discounted as actual crimes by the police, thus inflating the true crime rate somewhat.

As these technical difficulties in surveys are worked out in further research, greater confidence can be placed in reported rates of victimization. The results of improved surveys, moreover, are extremely valuable from both theoretical and practical standpoints. From a theoretical standpoint, it will become possible to relate experience as a victim to a variety of social background factors, such as income, education, religion, and race; and to a variety of psychological factors such as an individual's fears about crime, his attitudes toward the system of criminal justice, and his conception of himself as a citizen. It should be possible, in short, to shed light on the problem of whether some citizens are more prone than others to victimization by crime.

From a practical standpoint, accurate rates of victimization are essential for sensible police action and public policy relating to crime control. As matters now stand, a reported increase in crime rates may result when police are doing their job better by informing themselves about the extent of criminal activity, because the number of offenses known to the police is used as the primary basis for calculating the crime rate. Paradoxically, increased police effectiveness often initiates an increase in public criticism of the police, because of the rising official crime rates. In fact, the public response probably should be just the opposite. If it could be shown, however, that increased police activity also resulted in a decrease in rates of victimization, their effectiveness could be better gauged, and public approval and criticism more intelligently directed. Furthermore, if sociologists can provide measures of criminal activity (rates of victimization) that are independent of measures of work performed by the police (rates of offenses known to the police), the temptation of police agencies to manipulate their figures and protect their interest and public image would be lessened correspondingly. The use of the survey method to study crime therefore promises to ease a number of vexing tensions that characterize the relations between the police and the public in so many communities.

This illustration represents only one facet of the sociologist's abiding concern with the social and psychological origins of criminal activity, the prevention of crime, and the treatment of criminals once they are apprehended. While only part of the picture, however, the illustration reveals how an apparently simple problem of measurement intimately affects a whole range of conclusions we are likely to draw about the incidence of crime and police effectiveness in its control.

## A Study of Alienation among Workers

Is factory work in a capitalist society oppressive for working-men? What aspects of factory life are the most onerous? How will workers express dissatisfaction with their conditions of work?

These questions are old ones for sociologists, managers, workers, and policy-makers alike. A century ago Karl Marx (1818–83) argued force-fully that capitalist production resulted in a loss of control by the worker over his product and the processes of work, and a corresponding alienation of the worker from the system of production. This sense of alienation, Marx maintained, was one of the forces that pushed the worker toward revolutionary activity. Today, few social scientists would accept the radical Marxist position that alienation—and ultimately rev-olution—are the necessary consequences of the capitalist system of production. At the same time, however, many social scientists are seriously concerned with the psychological impact of factory life on workers and with consequences such as low morale, lack of political participation, and mental illness. This continuing interest is clearly merited, since satisfactions and dissatisfactions on the job are so impor-tant in understanding a variety of social problems, such as training workers for new technology, union-management relations, industrial strife, and the extent of alienation in the larger society.

One of the most careful sociological studies of worker dissatisfaction is Robert Blauner's *Alienation and Freedom,* published in 1964. Unlike many previous writers, Blauner did not treat alienation as a single en-tity, but rather distinguished among several of its ingredients. He identi-fied the components of *powerlessness,* which might arise when the worker does not control his means of production or work situation; *meaninglessness,* which might arise when the worker contributes only in small measure to the final product; *isolation,* which might arise when a worker does not belong to an effective social unit on the job; and *self-estrangement,* which arises when work becomes simply a means to make a living rather than a path toward individual self-fulfillment.

Blauner also assumed, unlike Marx, that factory conditions as such do not cause alienation, but rather that different types of industry give rise to different levels of dissatisfaction, because they have different technologies, different divisions of labor, different bureaucratic structures, and different positions in the economic structure. On the basis of this reasoning, he decided to study worker alienation in four industries that differed from one another along these dimensions—automobile production, textile production, automated chemical production, and printing. Using both his own and others' field research as data, he analyzed the structure of each industry, estimating which would be likely to produce an alienated work force. Then he checked these estimates against interviews of workers that yielded information on levels and types of dissatisfaction in each industry.

As expected, the auto workers were highest on alienation scores, and the printers lowest. On the assembly line, the auto worker has little control over his conditions of work, little relief from monotony, little responsibility for the total final product, little personal interaction on the job, and little involvement in a cohesive occupational community. By contrast, the printer, a member of one of the surviving crafts, sets his own pace of work, sees the results of his labor, works in a more intimate social setting, and belongs to an occupational community.

The textile workers expressed an intermediate level of alienation. As loom tenders they are subject to the same constraints as the automobile workers; they are tightly supervised, their pace of work is set, and they have almost as little control over the final product. The particular setting of the workers studied, however, was a small southern town with a traditional, homogeneous, and relatively stable social life, all of which probably counterbalanced the effects of the work situation. In a more urbanized setting, Blauner argued, these community ties would probably weaken, and the level of alienation would accordingly approach that of the auto workers.

Interestingly, the level of alienation among the operators in the chemical refinery was only slightly higher than among the printers. Though the operator does not determine the rate of continuous flow of production, he is responsible for monitoring it. He is often a member of a team, in which each member makes a definite contribution to the total work process, and he has some freedom to vary his style of work. He is not likely to be closely supervised by managers. These findings are most striking, for they suggest that, as automated processes are adopted in more industries, workers may become less rather than more alienated.

Blauner's research is also instructive from a methodological point of view. Rather than addressing the simple proposition that industrial capitalism gives rise to worker alienation, he approached the issue in a more complicated way. He identified several components of alienation, and several features of the work situation that might produce alienation. Then, using the method of systematic comparative illustration, he attempted to demonstrate the effects of the several determinants. By employing this research strategy he was able both to respect the complex and variable character of the social world and to continue the sociologist's search for social causes of attitude and behavior.

## A Survey of Intolerance

One sociological tool—the public opinion survey—has come to be such an important part of modern life that it is rare to find a magazine without a cartoon depicting some quixotic doorstep encounter between an earnest sociologist and an opinionated respondent. (Incidentally, the cartoon stereotype is inaccurate. Most interviewers are not male sociologists but housewives who work part time, and most scientific surveys are so detailed that they are conducted in the living room, not on the front steps.)

The best known form of opinion survey is the election poll, usually conducted during an election campaign to determine the relative strength of various candidates. These polls are of great interest to the mass media, to the candidates themselves, and to interested citizens. More complicated survey techniques can also be used to explore subtle and complex attitudes toward public issues. Samuel A. Stouffer's *Communism, Conformity, and Civil Liberties* is a well-known example of how surveys help to produce objective knowledge in situations in which "experts" may have totally misread popular opinion.

In the early 1950's—the era of "McCarthyism"—newspapers were filled with reports of subversion, investigations, and witch hunts to such an extent that responsible leaders were concerned about the presence of a national obsession that could threaten civil liberties. In this troubled atmosphere a private foundation commissioned Stouffer to direct a national survey to determine whether such an obsession existed.

The sampling and interviewing were conducted in 1954 by two national survey organizations, The American Institute of Public Opinion (The Gallup Poll) and the National Opinion Research Center (affiliated with the University of Chicago). The precision that well-designed surveys can attain was shown by the fact that the results from the two samples were almost identical.

Far from uncovering a "national hysteria," the data showed that the vast majority of Americans were not involved, one way or the other, in such issues of public policy. Thus, answers to the question "What kinds of things do you worry about most?" revealed that less than one percent of the 5,000 interviewees mentioned either the threat of Communists or threats to civil liberties. Most respondents mentioned more personal and immediate things, such as their health or their financial problems. This finding is even more astonishing when one notes that the bulk of the interviewing took place while the highly publicized "Army-McCarthy hearings" were in progress.

While the level of general concern was much less than one might expect, Stouffer's study did show a wide range of reactions to direct questions about Communists, Socialists, and persons questioned before congressional committees. Some Americans believed that any admitted Communists should be jailed, while others refused to accept the proposition that Communists should not be working in defense plants. Observing that the response to a number of such questions clustered statistically, Stouffer combined these responses to form an overall index of "Toleration of Non-Conformists." Then, through careful statistical analysis of many background variables, he developed a revealing picture of how the diverse social categories and social groups in modern America differ on tolerance.

Many of Stouffer's findings came as no surprise. For example, those living in rural areas and those living in the South showed more intolerance; educated people were more tolerant than uneducated ones; and young people were more tolerant than older people, even when allowance was made for the higher education of youth. Findings such as these led Stouffer to predict that levels of tolerance would increase as time goes on.

But some of his findings were startling. For example, few would expect any sex differences in tolerance, but Stouffer's analysis revealed that women are consistently less tolerant of Communists than men. Again, few would predict that commanders of American Legion posts and regents of chapters of the Daughters of the American Revolution would be tolerant of Communists. Yet a special sample of these types of community leaders showed their tolerance scores to be higher than the national average and higher than cross sections of their own communities (though lower than other leaders such as newspaper publishers or presidents of bar associations).

Perhaps the least obvious finding involved church attendance. Protestants and Catholics showed no general difference in tolerance. (Jews constituted too small a sample to provide reliable results.) But in both these major faiths regular church attenders were *less* tolerant than those who attended irregularly or not at all. This difference, moreover, could not be explained away by sex, age, educational, or regional factors. Stouffer did not claim to interpret this puzzling finding, but other parts of his research suggest a possible interpretation. In response to the question "What do Communists believe in?" 24 percent of the sample gave answers such as "against religion" as compared with smaller percentages for "government ownership of property" (18 percent) or "promoting domination of the world by Russia" (17 percent). This apparently religious basis of American opposition toward Communism is very striking, since many armchair interpreters had treated the issue of Communism in strictly political or economic terms.

## A Study of the Spread of a Wonder Drug

Is the modern world dominated by impersonal forces? Is it made up of isolated individuals whose decisions are manipulated by the media? Or do personal contacts still have a place in influencing people's behavior?

Many people associate assertions about overpowering social forces with sociology, and certainly much research has revealed the degree to which social structure conditions individual responses. Yet sociologists themselves are dubious of the omnipotence of these forces, largely because their own studies have shown the continuing importance of family, friends, and other interpersonal ties in determining a person's life activities.

At the simplest level, studies of family ties and friendship show that the contemporary urban American is not isolated, but has numerous friends and maintains close ties to a number of kinsmen. Of course, it is difficult to compare these findings with the past; we have no systematic surveys of friendship and family relations as they existed a century ago. But in the light of contemporary studies it can be concluded that Americans in the nineteenth century would have to have had a remarkable volume of social ties if there has been a striking decline. Indeed, since sociological studies show that rural families generally have smaller social circles than do urban ones, it might be that modern Americans are *less* socially isolated than they were in the old days.

In addition, sociologists have also produced a number of studies that document the extreme importance of personal influence on individual decisions. On behavior so diverse as movie attendance, adoption of new farming techniques, and voting for a presidential candidate, these studies have generally shown either that interpersonal influence is more important than the mass media or that the media have little effect unless the behavior is also supported by one's close associates.

One of the most sophisticated of these studies appeared in a book entitled *Medical Innovation,* by James S. Coleman, Elihu Katz, and Herbert Menzel. The study carries on a tradition of research on interpersonal influence associated with Columbia University's Bureau of Applied Social Research.

The authors were interested in whether, when, and under what conditions a doctor begins to prescribe a certain "wonder drug." To secure data they interviewed physicians in four medium-size cities. As a check on the reliability of the doctor's memory, they also meticulously inspected pharmacists' records to make certain of the exact date when a doctor began prescribing the drug.

Professional factors often influenced physicians' decisions to accept new techniques. The authors showed that the early adopters of the drug tended to be more frequent attenders of medical-specialty meetings, readers of more medical journals, and more recently trained.

The striking finding, however, concerns interpersonal influence. One of the strongest correlates of adoption of the drug is the number of times a doctor in a community is named by other doctors as a consultant on cases, an advisor, or a personal friend. Doctors who received more votes from their colleagues—those who are integrated into the inter-personal network of medicine—were among the first to try the medical innovation. Being hooked into the network was even a better predictor of adoption than having attended a high-prestige medical school.

By a complex series of mathematical analyses, the authors carried their study beyond the conclusion that personal contact and medical shop talk are important factors. Their data suggest that doctors who have many ties with other doctors become involved in a "snowball" pat-tern of adopting a new drug, whereas more isolated doctors reflect only a slow and steady increase in adoptions. The mechanism is this: If each doctor tells something to three other doctors and each of them relays that information to three others, and so on, the information spreads through the network with increasing velocity; whereas if each doctor makes up his mind on his own or tells only one other doctor, the diffu-sion process is much slower. The different rates of adoption as between the "personal influence" and the "isolated individual" patterns is shown graphically in Figure 1–2. The "chain-reaction" curve is a logistic curve similar to that produced by population-growth figures and autocatalytic chemical reactions. The "snowball" effect in interpersonal networks, in short, are similar to the effects claimed for the famous "chain letters."

In these ways the structure of interpersonal networks helps to deter-mine the decision process, even for "strictly scientific" decisions that one would expect to be influenced almost solely by medical-journal com-munication or drug-company advertising. Ironically, Coleman, Katz, and Menzel suggested that the best way to think about the spread of this medical innovation is as an epidemic.

This study reveals a great deal about how doctors pick up their ideas. It suggests that personal influence makes for a much faster rate of adoption of new techniques than would result from formal mechanisms of communication alone. It also suggests that in some cases "fads" may spread through medical circles by word of mouth before they have been systematically tested. Finally, the study probably tells us a great deal about how attitudes are formed in the general populace—attitudes toward child-rearing, dieting, movie stars, or foreign nations, for in-stance. The better we understand informal channels of communication, in short, the more light we can throw on the problem of how ideas shape human behavior.

## A Pioneer Investigation of Marihuana Users

During the past few years the use of marihuana by young people has appeared to increase dramatically throughout the country. At

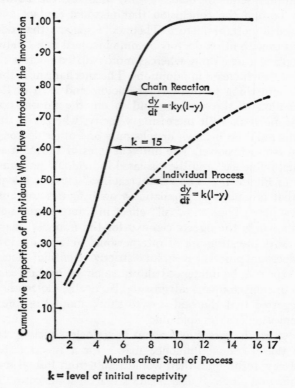

**k = level of initial receptivity**

**FIGURE 1-2   COMPARISON OF MODEL OF CHAIN-REACTION INNOVATION WITH MODEL OF INDIVIDUAL INNOVATION, ASSUMING THE SAME RECEPTIVITY**

Source:   Reprinted from James S. Coleman, Elihu Katz, and Herbert Menzel, *Medical Innovation: A Diffusion Study* (Indianapolis: Bobbs-Merril Co., 1966), Figure 27, p. 99 by permission of the publisher.

the same time the concern with its use on the part of law-enforcement authorities and the public at large has also increased. Yet knowledge of the phenomenon lags far behind the concern. The citizen is beset by contradictory claims about the extent of the use of marihuana, the reasons for its use, the characteristics of its users, and its effect in the short and long run. This confusion reflects how little is known with certainty.

Long before the public became concerned, a few sociologists had begun to examine various kinds of drug use. In a pioneering study conducted fifteen years ago, Howard S. Becker attempted to discover whether there were any uniform experiences that people underwent as they became habitual users of marihuana. Like a medical investigator studying the natural history of a disease, Becker was interested in discovering a typical beginning, course of development, reactions to symptoms, and peak or decline of the use of marihuana.

All the people studied passed through a similar sequence of experiences before they learned to use marihuana for pleasure. First, if genuine effects were to be experienced, the novice had to learn the technique of smoking. People did not usually get "high" when they first tried marihuana. Several attempts, usually following the instruction or example of an experienced user, were essential. Second, the user had to learn to recognize the effects and connect them with drug use. Becker's interviews revealed, surprisingly, that an individual might display the recognizable physical symptoms of being "high" without actually recognizing these effects himself. People were often taught by experienced users to recognize the symptoms associated with the drug. Third, the user had to learn to enjoy the sensations after he had learned to recognize them. At first dizziness, tingling scalp, and distortions of time and distance were ambiguous or frightening. Again, experienced users often helped the novice, by reassurance and shared experience, to overcome the negative reactions and redefine the sensations as pleasurable.

Becker's work is a good example of a study that cannot be guided by the usual canons of quantification and rigorous research design. Because the use of marihuana is surrounded by social taboos, the investigator finds it difficult to locate users who will give information freely to an impersonal observer. As a result, a standard questionnaire survey of a sample of the population simply would not turn up very revealing data. When sociologists study highly private matters such as sex or crime, they have to devise more informal ways of locating subjects and securing information. Furthermore, when the investigator deals with an unfamiliar or deviant kind of behavior, he must gain a sympathetic appreciation of the behavior—through extended observation and conversation with his subjects—to be certain he does not ascribe a conventional meaning to the behavior when it does not apply.

In his study Becker located fifty marihuana users by whatever means he could, making certain that the subjects represented a variety of social backgrounds and social roles. The users were often contacted through referral by persons whose confidence Becker had already secured, so they would speak candidly. The subjects were asked to describe in detail how they came to use the drug and how they used it in the present. To encourage the free flow of new information, and to avoid misinterpretations, the subjects were encouraged to tell the story in their own way, with extensive informal probing by the interviewer.

If Becker had used more "scientific" procedures—such as the standardized questionnaire—in his study, he might not have been so successful in locating marihuana users or discovering the regularities in its use. Moreover, this point applies to many kinds of behavior other than the private, the touchy, and the taken-for-granted. It is essential that both sociologists and the larger public recognize the importance of this informal style of research, and that training and support for it not be overlooked in the drive to encourage more rigorous, standardized methods. Even though the findings that are based on informal methods are relatively "soft" from a methodological point of view, they often provide the basic hypotheses—as Becker's study has done—for subsequent, more highly controlled research.

## A Study of Group Membership in Disaster Situations

How do people react when a disaster, such as a tornado or an explosion, strikes a community? Why do some panic, while others try to rescue those in distress, and still others rush to join loved ones? Does a person experience a conflict of loyalties in crisis situations, and, if so, how does he react to the conflict?

Such were some of the questions that guided the research of a number of social scientists at the University of Oklahoma Research Institute as they interviewed citizens of four southwestern communities that had been stricken by tornadoes in the late 1940's. These investigators worked from a few initial assumptions. First, they acknowledged that all citizens in a community are normally involved in a number of different roles— for example, husband, fireman, member of the Baptist church, member of the Democratic party, member of an Elks Lodge, and so on. These roles call for different and sometimes conflicting kinds of behavior. Second, the investigators acknowledge that an individual builds a number of loyalties toward the groups to which his roles attach him—to his family, his work organization, his church, his political party, and his voluntary association. Third, they were aware that the routine of daily life usually minimizes conflicts between these various roles. The week is scheduled, for example, to permit the citizen to fulfill his loyalties to these various groups at different times; and behavior appropriate to one role is frequently separated geographically from behavior appropriate to others. But finally, they assumed that when a catastrophe strikes a community, these conflict-reducing influences are disrupted, and the individual is faced with a perplexing question: Which role should guide his behavior? Should he behave as husband, fireman, or member of the community at large?

The results of the interviews, reported by Lewis Killian, indicated that such role-conflicts occupied a very important place in determining behavior in crisis situations though the individuals involved were not always conscious of the conflict at the time.

The most common conflict was between the family and other groups, especially the employment group or the community at large. Policemen, firemen, and public-utility workers faced the question of whether to leave their work place and return to their families or friends, or carry out essential leadership roles in meeting the crisis. Others not in such central roles faced a decision as to whether to join loved ones or to rescue and give relief to distressed strangers. In most cases, the question was resolved in favor of the family or friendship group, though there were also many cases of individuals who knew their families and friends were safe and who thus could stay at their posts.

A second type of conflict was between carrying out an essentially occupational role and the "heroic role" of rescuer. A minister, for example, was torn between consoling families of victims and going to the disaster area to help rescue the stricken. Others, such as public-utility workers, experienced conflict because the routine performance of their duties required them to disregard the plight of injured citizens. A few community members experienced a third type of conflict, between the loyalty of employees to "the company" as an organization and to fellow employees as friends and human beings. Finally, a few individuals discovered that there was a conflict between their loyalty to the community and their loyalty to some extra-community group. Some telephone workers on strike, for instance, experienced conflicts between loyalty to the union, which would have kept them off the job, and loyalty to the stricken community, which would have drawn them back to work in the disaster area. In one case, workers remained on strike but were criticized harshly by their fellow townsmen.

These kinds of research findings are instructive in several ways. They indicate the relative strength of an individual's several group loyalties, and indicate how he will typically behave when he is forced to choose among them. In addition they suggest to community leaders the kinds of complications that may arise in a community's response to disaster, particularly if individuals in key leadership positions are subjected to critical conflicts of group loyalty. And finally, from the standpoint of planning, these results suggest the need to assign responsibility—in advance of crises—for the care of dependents when disaster strikes, and the need to communicate—quickly and authoritatively—information to disaster workers concerning the welfare of their dependents at times of crisis. In short, such findings, if strengthened and consolidated by further research, are indispensable for those who must plan for disaster and mobilize people when it occurs.

## Comparative Study of Occupational Prestige

Do countries—the United States, the Soviet Union, and Japan, for instance—become more similar to one another as they continue to industrialize? Or do their differences become more pronounced? Do the forces of urbanization and industrialization overwhelm distinctive cultural outlooks and traditions, or do these persist despite rapid social change? Such questions preoccupy many of the scholars whose special interest is economic development.

One way to throw light on the matter is to study how different countries evaluate occupations within their societies. One possible argument is that because all industrializing countries have introduced a common economic system—factory production and mass distribution—they have created a large number of similar occupations, such as engineer, manager, factory-worker, and salesman. Furthermore, the argument goes, because these occupations require approximately the same levels of skill and responsibility in all countries, they are given about the same levels of prestige in all countries. The conclusion from this reasoning is that, as countries industrialize, they evolve toward systems of occupational prestige that resemble one another. The other possibility is that the traditional value-systems of different countries influence the ranking of occupations even in the face of industrialization. Because the United States has a cultural heritage that places high value on business success, for example, we would rank business managers higher than, say, the French, who have traditionally valued other kinds of social activity more highly than economic success. The conclusion from this reasoning is that, despite evolving similarities of occupational structure, industrial countries will continue to differ from one another in systems of occupational prestige.

The first systematic comparative study of occupational prestige was published by Alex Inkeles and Peter Rossi in 1956. They were able to locate a number of surveys that had been conducted in the United States, Great Britain, New Zealand, Japan, Germany, and—by using the results of interviews with displaced persons—the Soviet Union. In each of these surveys respondents were asked to evaluate a large number of occupations in relation to one another. From these responses a prestige score or an average rank was calculated for each occupation. Inkeles and Rossi were hindered in their analysis by the fact that the various surveys were administered under different conditions. Nevertheless, they found it possible to compare the relative rankings of different occupations in these six advanced countries.

The results showed a striking similarity of occupational rankings. Inkeles and Rossi asked how strongly correlated were the prestige scores or average ranks of the occupations that appeared in all the national surveys. The correlation coefficients are presented in Table 1-1. Twelve of the fifteen coefficients are above .9—which is remarkably high—and only one is below .8. Correlation coefficients with a value of 1.0 signify a perfect association; those with a value of 0 signify no association. On the basis of these and other strong indications, Inkeles and Rossi concluded that "despite the heterogeneity in research design, there exists among the six nations a marked degree of agreement on the relative prestige of matched occupations." Occasional occupations showed a discrepancy—for example, a company director was rated higher in Japan than in the United States, a clergyman was rated higher in the United States than in Great Britain or Japan—but no definite pattern of disagreement among nations appeared in agriculture or "service" (barber, chef, shoe shiner), both of which are difficult to assimilate to an industrial ranking system. Inkeles and Rossi concluded from these findings that "there is a relatively invariable hierarchy of prestige associated with the industrial system." The findings also suggest a convergence toward some common occupational-ranking system as nations industrialize.

Later and more comprehensive studies, however, have thrown some doubt on these interpretations. By 1966 enough additional survey data had accumulated to permit Robert W. Hodge, Donald J. Treiman, and Peter H. Rossi to make a similar comparative analysis of surveys from

**TABLE 1-1   CORRELATIONS BETWEEN PRESTIGE SCORES (OR RANKS) GIVEN TO COMPARABLE OCCUPATIONS IN SIX NATIONAL STUDIES**

|  | U.S.S.R. | Japan | Great Britain | New Zealand | U.S. | Germany* |
|---|---|---|---|---|---|---|
| U.S.S.R. | – | .74 | .83 | .83 | .90 | .90 |
| Japan | .74 | – | .92 | .91 | .93 | .93 |
| Great Britain | .83 | .92 | – | .97 | .94 | .97 |
| New Zealand | .83 | .91 | .97 | – | .97 | .96 |
| United States | .90 | .93 | .94 | .97 | – | .96 |
| Av. correlation | .84 | .89 | .93 | .93 | .94 | .94 |

Source: Alex Inkeles and Peter Rossi, "National Comparisons of Occupational Prestige," *American Journal of Sociology,* 61 (1956), Table 2, 332. Reprinted by permission of the University of Chicago Press.

* All coefficients are product-moment correlations, with the exception of those involving Germany, which are rank-order coefficients. The average number of identical or similar occupations on which the correlations were calculated was 17.

24 countries, many of which were non-Western and relatively non-industrialized (for example, Indonesia and Ghana). The results of this study showed that the occupational-ranking systems of not only the industrialized societies *but also the non-industrialized ones* greatly resemble one another. The average coefficients of all non-farm occupations for all the nations studied was .83, which is very similar to the average of .88 observed in the United States and the five other countries by Inkeles and Rossi. From these and other findings, Hodge, Treiman and Rossi argued that neither industrialization nor level of economic development apparently determines the similarity among occupational-prestige systems, but that these similarities may rest on more general structural requirements shared by all complex societies.

Taken together, the two studies underscore the need for both theoretical and methodological improvements in the comparative study of prestige systems, as well as of other social phenomena. At the theoretical level, a sharper statement of the general requirements of complex social systems—as well as the special requirements of industrial systems—must be formulated, to permit consistent interpretation of both gross similarities and fine differences. Both studies were plagued with methodological problems. The occupational categories differed from survey to survey; the number of occupations differed; the questions were worded differently; different coding and ranking systems were employed by different investigators; different samples were tapped in different countries; and the surveys were conducted at different points in time. The studies were hindered methodologically, in short, because they had to rely on data that "happened" to be created under very different circumstances in a number of countries. The data would be vastly improved if fifty or sixty nations, varying culturally and according to degree of industrialization, could be surveyed in a standardized manner with a standardized list of occupations. This kind of systematization of research methods is essential if we are to gain confidence in comparative data.

### Comparative Study of Changes in the Family

What impact has industrialization and urbanization had on family life throughout the world during the past 200 years? Is the family disintegrating? Or is it simply changing its structure in order to perform its functions more effectively in modern society?

These are among the most persistent questions posed by sociologists of the family. Unfortunately, however, the history of inquiry into these questions has yielded many simplified generalizations about the rise in the divorce rate, the decline of parental authority, and the decline of the extended family structure during and after the Industrial Revolution in the West.

In the past few decades these simplified views have been challenged. Some investigators have attempted to demonstrate that what is seen as "modern" family life—an egalitarian, isolated, nuclear family—actually has antedated industrialization and urbanization in many cases. Others have pointed out that countries with different starting-points, such as Japan or India, experience different historical changes in their family structures. Others have suggested that, while demands of modern society make for some changes in family life, such as high mobility of families, various forms of the extended family persist because of improvements in transportation and communication. These improvements permit continued contact among extended family members even though geographical distances among them are greater than before.

The most important comparative research on changes in family structure was reported in 1963 in William J. Goode's book, *World Revolution and Family Patterns*. This study is considerably more advanced than other research on family change. It is broader in comparative scope, including data on Arabic Islam, Sub-Saharan Africa, India, China, and Japan, as well as the modern West. Moreover, it is more carefully rooted in empirical data, relying on masses of surveys, censuses, registration data, and community studies, as well as less systematic descriptions.

Goode's main proposition is that the social forces of industrialization and urbanization are working to produce a single type of family system —the conjugal system—which has fewer ties with distant relatives and greater emphasis on the nuclear family. Most of his research was designed to document this generalization; but he qualified his argument in a number of ways. First, he noted that because family changes occur in many different types of socio-cultural milieux, they converge toward the ideal-typical conjugal family structure at different rates of speed. Second, he stressed that because the traditional family systems in various regions differ so much from one another, the paths toward this common convergence might move in different directions. For example, one region with traditionally high divorce rates (Arab Islam) may be moving toward a rate that ultimately will be similar to that of another region (Western Europe) with traditionally low divorce rates, although for a long period the movement of their respective rates may be in opposite directions. Third, Goode noted different rates of change within any given society, with the consequence that social-class and other internal differences in family structure may persist for long periods. Finally, while emphasizing industrialization as the main causal factor, he also acknowledged the importance of other causal factors—especially ideologies such as egalitarianism—and acknowledged that the family itself may be an agent of economic and social change.

Within this framework, Goode proceeded to amass enormous quantities of data concerning world trends in marriage rates, courtship patterns, inheritance and property laws, premarital behavior, extended kinship, illegitimacy, divorce, the social position of women, and numerous other topics. In interpreting these data, he consistently viewed the statistical and historical trends in each region as results of a tension between forces attributable to the peculiar cultural traditions of that region and the forces attributable to urban-industrial change.

While impressive by comparison with other studies of the family, Goode's research is nevertheless burdened with a number of problems. Some of these problems are conceptual and theoretical. For example, while specifying several plausible effects of industrialization and urbanization on the family, he admits that it is not at all clear "how industrialization or urbanization affects the family system, or how the family system facilitates or hinders these processes." To sort out these complex processes, it is necessary to characterize the major variables more precisely. Certainly the probable impact of industrialization should be separated conceptually from the probable impact of urbanization. Furthermore, neither industrialization nor urbanization constitutes an irreducible whole. Several subtypes of each—for example, heavy versus light industry, extractive versus manufacturing industry, small versus large plant—should be identified for purposes of comparative analysis. In addition, it is advisable to classify the possible historical outcomes of the interplay of social forces in terms more complex than "the conjugal family." Several variants should be specified to refine the analysis. Introducing this kind of complexity on both sides of the causal network permits us more readily to establish the specific conditions under which Goode's various propositions should hold.

Other problems are methodological and empirical. Goode himself observed that the measures he used—censuses, attitude surveys, descriptive accounts, and the like—are by no means standardized or equally available for different societies. Consequently, the investigator is not certain of the validity of his data or the correctness of the inferences drawn from them. Moreover, even when adequate data are available, they cover such a short time period that the investigator is seldom aware whether he is viewing a long-term trend or a short-term fluctuation of data on the family. Such problems underscore the twin needs—equally urgent—for theoretical refinement and empirical research based on standardized comparative measures. These needs must be met if knowledge of the causes of changes in family life are to become more scientifically grounded.

## THE FRAMEWORK OF SOCIOLOGY

Though we have been selective in presenting these vignettes of sociologists at work, one conclusion seems inescapable: Sociology is both broad and diverse. It has developed a long list of subdivisions, an array of research methods, and a proliferation of schools of thought and theoretical approaches. How can we encompass this diversity within a general body of ideas? What are sociology's major conceptual tools? What is its distinctive framework?

### Sociological Perspectives

In reviewing the research and teaching of sociologists, we have extracted five aspects of social life that constitute the major perspectives of sociology.

The first is the *demographic* and *ecological* aspect. This involves explaining regularities and variations in the behavior of human organisms, located in space and time and situated in a physical and biological environment. The main preoccupations of demography and ecology are explaining patterns of birth, death, migration, spatial arrangement, and related characteristics of human populations.

The second aspect is the concern of the long-standing field of social psychology. This involves explaining behavior in terms of its *psychological* significance to human organisms, considered as selves or persons. The psychological system of the individual is made up of his motives, cognitions, skills, social attitudes, and sense of identity. While this perspective is obviously shared with the discipline of psychology, it has a solid place in sociology as well. Social psychologists investigate a wide array of topics, including interaction patterns in small groups, the formation of attitudes, the interplay of society and personality in processes of socialization, and the formation and dissemination of beliefs during episodes of collective behavior.

These two aspects focus on the individual organism. A third aspect of social life—the *collective* aspect—emerges when we consider aggregated numbers of individuals who form groups or organizations with common purposes. When sociologists study primary groups, voluntary associations, formal organizations, or even whole societies, they usually regard them as collectivities of persons considered as members involved in different patterns of interaction. Sometimes sociologists study groups and organizations as units in their own right, without reference to their individual members—as in studies of competition among political parties, conflict among racial groups, or status-striving among cliques.

A fourth and different perspective arises when social life is regarded not from the standpoint of the persons involved, but from the standpoint of *structural relations* that arise in the course of their interaction. The concept of "role" characterizes these relations—for example, the roles of husband and wife, politician and voter, employer and employee, businessman and consumer. "Person" and "role" are analytically separate concepts. A person occupies many different roles; a role cannot refer to a complete person, but only to selected aspects of his behavior. The concept of "social structure" refers to patterns of roles organized around the fulfillment of some social function—for example, religious structure, educational structure, or political structure.

The fifth aspect concerns a variety of *cultural* phenomena that regulate, legitimize, and lend meaning to social behavior. Norms, for example, are standards that regulate interactions among persons and groups. An illustration is the network of contract laws that govern market interchange. Values, another component of culture, are standards that provide legitimacy for social arrangements. An example is the value of "equality of opportunity," which has served as the legitimizing basis for many American institutions throughout our history. Finally, ideologies and cosmologies provide a context within which values and norms are grounded in meaning. Illustrations are religious belief systems, such as Christianity, and the ideological beliefs associated with social movements, such as socialism.

The subject matter of sociology, then, is found in the demographic-ecological, social-psychological, collective, structural, and cultural aspects of social life. The sociological enterprise is to explain regularities, variations, and interdependencies among these aspects. This enterprise has both a static and a dynamic aspect. Sometimes sociologists ask why patterns of organized social life persist, but equally often they are concerned with processes of social change, which destroy old social forms and create new ones.

In practice, these several aspects of sociology are not so neatly set off from one another as a simple summary might imply. Sometimes a sociologist studies more than one aspect, and occasionally he ventures into territories other than those we have mentioned. Moreover, in identifying these aspects, we do not wish to convey the impression that the scope of sociology is fixed or static. Sociologists continuously attempt to redefine and refine the central aspects of sociological study; new fields and emphases rise and fall; and some parts of the discipline, such as demography, show signs of separating and crystallizing as separate disciplines. The history of sociology is noted for its dynamism, its tendency to spin off in various directions. We have no reason to believe that the future will not show the same diversity and vitality.

## Sociological Explanation

So much for the aspects of social life that sociologists try to explain. How do they go about the job of explaining regularities and variations in social phenomena? The type of sociological explanation that appears least complicated is the hypothesis—a statement of the

logically and presumably temporally prior conditions under which behavior may be expected to vary in certain ways. A simple sociological
hypothesis is: The level of violence committed by members of a group
varies directly with the level of economic deprivation experienced by the
group. In this case behavior is accounted for by referring to group
membership and the group's position in the social structure.

Closer examination reveals, however, that even simple hypotheses of
this sort involve a number of ancillary assertions, assumptions, and perspectives. Consider the hypothesis just stated. Taken at face value, the
hypothesis implies that economic hardship has a direct affect on a group
and its members. This assertion is questionable on psychological
grounds, since different groups have different levels of susceptibility to
economic hardship; and, within any group, individuals bring different
meanings to economic hardships and have different thresholds of tolerance. Furthermore, the hypothesis implies a number of psychological
variables—such as frustration and aggression—that intervene between
economic hardship and violent behavior. Finally, the sociologist may be
aware that variables other than the level of economic hardship affect
violence. In addition, hardship produces a number of responses other
than violence—for example, rationalization or resignation. For all these
reasons, it is evident that a simple hypothesis invariably involves a
whole family of statements that stand in some implicit relation to one
another. Put another way, any single hypothesis relates to a system of
hypotheses. Put still another way, any hypothesis implies a *model* or
*theory* of behavior. Furthermore, the roots of the model or theory are
to be found, once again, in the various frameworks—demographic,
ecological, psychological, collective, structural, and cultural—that constitute the substance of sociology.

## Sociological Theories

If this is the case, what is the distinctive character of sociological theory? We view sociological theory in its explanatory sense. Theory makes explicit the variables and relations that are often only implicit
in hypotheses, and sets these ingredients into some logical—including
mathematical—relation with one another. The specialist in empirical
research looks toward the facts, and proceeds to locate, measure, and

record data; to assure the reliability and relevance of these data; and to control other possible variables by experimental, statistical, or other techniques. The specialist in theory looks toward the conceptual context of the hypothesis. He considers such issues as the mutual exclusiveness and logical exhaustiveness of classes of variables and relations; the internal consistency of hypotheses; their consistency with other bodies of knowledge; their economy of expression; and their power to generate new hypotheses when combined with other assumptions and assertions.

Two broad strategies for constructing theories are identifiable in contemporary sociology. The first, by far the most common, is to capture the complexity of the social world by constructing rather loosely knit verbal frameworks. An example is the theory of the German-Italian theorist, Robert Michels (1876–1936), who argued that, because of certain features of large organizations, and because of certain psychological characteristics of leaders and followers, all social organizations are subject to an "iron law of oligarchy," by virtue of which a ruling elite develops and true democracy becomes impossible. Another example is the theoretical work of Talcott Parsons (1902–　), who has attempted to identify all the theoretically significant components of social interaction, and to set these components into systematic relations with one another. Such verbal theories have the advantage of being easily applicable to a wide range of empirical phenomena. However, they often fall short of desired scientific rigor.

The second strategy of theory construction is to design very simplified and abstract mathematical versions of social structures and processes. This strategy has the advantage of affording the opportunity for deductive reasoning, thereby making it possible to trace the implications of a set of assumptions and to check the internal consistency of a set of propositions. However, these mathematical formulations often require that the empirical world be made over-simple and unreal. In principle the verbal and the mathematical approaches complement each other; mathematics may be used to systematize a loose verbal structure, or verbal interpretations may relate mathematical discoveries to the observable world. In practice, however, there is often a tension between the verbal and mathematical strategies—a tension between realistic, but possibly loose, scientifically inadequate formulations, and elegant, scientifically rigorous, but possibly unrealistic theories. It is too early to foresee which strategy will ultimately be more fruitful for sociology.

Among the small minority of sociologists who use mathematical models, there is little agreement on the most fruitful type of mathematical approach. No single approach has proven sufficiently applicable to merit its widespread acceptance in the discipline. In general, however, mathematical sociologists fall into two roughly defined groups: those who use modern algebra, topology, lattice theory, and other abstract tools of modern mathematics; and those who stress more traditional forms of mathematics and statistics, such as ordinary algebra, calculus, probability, and applied multivariate statistical analysis. The differences between the two groups are partly matters of theoretical preference, but generational differences are also important. Modern techniques are used by those who have been trained recently, while traditional forms of mathematics are used more often by older sociologists.

Sociologists who use modern mathematical techniques focus mainly on networks of communication and interpersonal relations—for example, in small groups or bureaucracies. Some mathematical studies of kinship have been made. Graph theory has figured in a recent work on balance theory in social psychology and sociometry. Such mathematical approaches are also suited for drawing inferences about interaction in complex situations involving multiple roles, levels of authority, and subgroups—all of which concern structural as well as social-psychological relations among persons and groups.

Sociologists who use the more traditional mathematical tools have been less systematic, in that they have attempted to explain known relationships among empirical data. For example, mathematical models of change have been used to describe processes of diffusion. Differential equations have been applied to patterns of population growth. Probability models have been used to characterize occupational mobility between generations, and to estimate the points at which an occupational distribution will stabilize. Techniques of multivariate statistical analysis, long used in economics and biology, have been applied to sociological problems. Path analysis has been used to ascertain whether different factors are at work in the occupational histories of Negroes and whites.

One final comment on sociological theory is in order. Whether it be verbal or mathematical, it is clear that theory borders closely on logic and epistemology, as well as morals and politics. Any set of sociological principles rests on philosophical notions concerning inference, causality, and scientific truth. Furthermore, sociology overlaps with religious, moral, and political doctrines because all involve general assertions about man's relation to man. A consequence of this is that much of what is called "theoretical analysis" in sociology is, in fact, an effort to relate the work of a sociological theorist to some epistemological, moral, or political position. Some of the most heated theretical controversies in sociology concern the philosophical or ideological foundations of a theory rather than its explanatory utility. We prefer an emphasis on the latter, but many sociologists would not concur. In any case, given sociology's kinship with political and moral preoccupations, it is reasonable to expect that scientific sociology will not soon be separated from man's propensity to politicize and moralize.

# 2
# DEVELOPING AREAS OF SOCIOLOGY

We now consider sociology in terms of its developmental trends, its probable future, and its problems and needs. Once again we must be selective. We cannot hope to present a complete picture of the past accomplishments, present status, and future prospects for every field in the discipline. Sociology is much too complex and fluid to permit that kind of effort. Instead, we have selected an illustrative sample of different patterns of growth in various fields.

We begin by considering research methods. First, we shall consider the variety of methods in sociology, and the kinds of service each has given the discipline. Second, we shall consider the comparative study of societies, an endeavor that does not necessarily require unique research methods, but that has some special theoretical and methodological problems that merit attention.

Next we shall turn to four sets of substantive fields, grouped somewhat arbitrarily:

(1) Three fields that are widely agreed to have shown solid theoretical and empirical accomplishments—demography, social stratification, and complex organizations.

(2) Three fields that are especially concerned with social and psychological dynamics—socialization, deviance and social control, and social change.

(3) Three fields that focus on important institutional complexes

and have displayed unusually great activity since World War II—political sociology, the sociology of education, and medical sociology.

(4) Two fields that have remained at a relatively low level of development in theory and research because of a peculiar combination of obstacles—the sociology of religion and the sociology of race relations.

## RESEARCH METHODS IN SOCIOLOGY: TRENDS AND NEEDS

In the past fifty years sociologists have made increasing use of standardized methods of collecting data and quantitative methods of analyzing them. The scientific quality of sociological research and training has improved accordingly. This trend toward methodological sophistication, however, has been slowed by two important factors: the unsatisfactory quality of many of the data sociologists are able to collect, and the inadequate mathematical and statistical training of the average sociologist.

### The Variety of Research Methods

Prior to 1940, most sociologists—conducting their studies alone and with limited resources—relied on informal methods. Many of the major empirical studies were based on "participant observation," in which the investigator immersed himself in a social setting to study it intensively. In one study, Nels Anderson investigated the world of the hobo by actually becoming one. In another, William F. Whyte studied social processes in lower-class "slum" street-corner groups by joining and talking informally with members of the groups.

Sociologists still use informal research methods when they study situations about which little is known or situations in which everyday behavior is so familiar that it is likely to be taken for granted. Some recent examples are studies of the jazz musician, marihuana users (see the vignette in Chapter 1 on Howard S. Becker's research), and the Black Muslim movement. Studies of this sort are often extraordinarily rich in original insights that would have been difficult to obtain through more formal methods, such as survey research or experimentation. Their results suffer, however, from lack of generalizability, since they are based on small samples of carefully selected respondents. Many sociologists argue that such studies are essential for developing hypotheses, but inadequate for testing them.

Data for a number of early studies of American community life—such as the *Middletown* and *Yankee City* series—were gathered as investigators took up residence in the community and interviewed many of its citizens. Still other studies made use of personal documents, such as letters and autobiographies; a classic example is *The Polish Peasant in Europe and America*, by W. I. Thomas and Florian Znaniecki, which contributed greatly to our understanding of immigrant minorities.

The small-group experiment, a method that has enjoyed a long history in psychology, is also employed by sociological investigators. Typically a group of paid undergraduates are brought together and assigned some sort of task for one or more meetings. As they interact, investigators record and analyze their behavior. While caution should be exercised in generalizing from experimental situations to natural situations—and generalizing from college students to people in general—much can be learned from such experiments, especially if they deal with general problems, such as the emergence of different types of leaders or the control of deviant behavior. Under experimental conditions, too, certain variables can be conveniently manipulated; for example, a "stooge," who has been coached to act in some deviant way, is introduced into a group to study how its members will react to him. A final advantage is that the small-group experiment, unlike many other types of research, is relatively inexpensive and is easily replicated. Investigators making use of these techniques must be sensitive, however, to the many ethical problems involved in concealing the purposes of the experiment from one or more subjects.

Experimental small-group research appears to be becoming increasingly quantitative and systematic. Most investigators take great care in measuring and recording behavior in experimental situations. Refined statistical methods and mathematical models have been used extensively in analyzing group processes, and some investigators are attempting computer simulation of group processes as a way of developing hypotheses. Still others have become interested in studying small groups by direct observation in natural settings, to overcome the objection that experiments are artificial and not generalizable to other situations.

The most common type of empirical research in sociology is the survey, including enumerative surveys and sample surveys of populations. These surveys are used in the study of many different variables, such as the attitudes, opinions, and behavior of some defined population, or the attributes of its organized life. The main reason for the extensive development of the sample survey is that it provides a manageable and efficient design for collecting data and for generalizing to larger populations. The large-scale survey has made possible the use of statistical analyses, including the techniques of multivariate analysis. (See, for example, the vignette in Chapter 1 on the attitudes toward communism.) By using such techniques, an investigator interested in race prejudice can *simultaneously* assess the influence of variables such as occupation, income, and age on racial attitudes. He may also employ mathematical models to represent causal relationships among variables.

Large-scale surveys, however, have limitations. Often questions to be asked in a standard way of many people have to be relatively superficial, and sociologists are aware of the need to conduct lengthy interviews in depth to appreciate the psychological context of many attitudes. But such interviews involving different individuals are very expensive and difficult to make comparable. Also, sociologists recognize that, ideally, respondents should be studied over long periods of time to trace changes in their attitudes; most surveys simply record attitudes at given moments. But again, longitudinal studies are expensive, difficult from a practical standpoint because of the necessity to trace respondents over long periods of time, and questionable ethically because of the burdens placed on respondents. One type of longitudinal design is the "panel survey," in which at least some members of a sample are interviewed over two or more time intervals to assess changes in their attitudes and behavior.

## Unresolved Problems and Needs

With the growth of survey research and the application of sophisticated statistical techniques to survey data, sociologists have become increasingly aware of the importance of accurate measurement and the necessity of gathering data that are comparable from one study to the next. As matters now stand, too few studies are based on genuinely comparable data. Too few studies are repeated in different situations, and too little attention is given to the development of measures that can be reported in the same way in different studies. This problem exists in part because sociologists do not always report their research procedures well. More importantly, it exists because research has to be carried out on such a small scale. In the past, sociologists conducted their own survey projects with little or no outside financing. At present, research teams obtain funds for larger studies, but each team tends to work independently from the next, asking different questions and using different measures. Because these studies are rarely comparable with one another, sociologists have been unable to take full advantage of the large number of available multivariate statistical techniques.

When entire communities or societies—as opposed to individuals—are the units of analysis, the problem of comparability of data is even more severe. It is feasible to survey many thousands of individuals. But comparable surveys of communities are often much more expensive, and often investigators must compare data that have been collected for other purposes. Sociologists make extensive use of United States census data when comparing cities, counties, and states with one another; but too often they do not find the kinds of information they most need in these sources. The investigator who wishes to compare different societies faces even greater handicaps. Often he must use indirect measures for comparisons, and the comparisons are often suspect because the data have been collected in such different ways and are embedded in such different cultural contexts.

The problem of the availability of appropriate data is a general one in sociology. The discipline—in contrast to economics, for instance—is not at present blessed by theoretically relevant data produced by the established recording procedures of society. Many of the economist's data are available to him because they are recorded in market transactions, stock exchange reports, and government statistics. These data come to him relatively inexpensively. In a greater proportion of cases the sociologist is forced either to rely on distorted approximations of data gathered for some other purpose than his own (in which case the data are likely to be unreliable) or he must make his own data by conducting surveys or otherwise gathering fresh information (in which case the data are likely to be very expensive). Sociologists should be prepared to build these additional costs into their research planning, and those who support sociologists in their research should be alerted to this feature of sociological investigation. Many sociological research projects are very costly. But it should be kept in mind that this fact is traceable not so much to some willful extravagance of the sociologist as to the fact that the cost of locating and acquiring new data is manifestly greater than the cost of relying on already available data.

These concerns suggest the need for establishing new and systematic ways of gathering standardized and sociologically relevant data that can be made widely available for social-scientific research. In Chapter 6 we venture some recommendations for improving the data base for sociology.

At present, the discipline of sociology is not well organized for ambitious cooperative research. In part, this is traceable to the departmental organization of universities. Most departments are composed of sociologists with diverse interests, to provide a balanced training program for students. Thus, sociologists interested in a single type of research—for example, delinquency—cannot gather in a single department, because the department seeks diversity and balance. They are scattered throughout the country, with only limited opportunities to interact with one another for sustained periods. Large-scale research, as a consequence, has been conducted not in departments but in specialized research centers. These circumstances suggest the need for new institutional research arrangements—such as inter-university research consortia—and for more and better ways for specialists to communicate with one another.

The mushrooming of interest in survey research and quantitative methods has produced a number of problems for graduate training programs in sociology. First, these methods may be displacing other valuable research methods in graduate curricula, such as participant observation and the study of historical archives, which are not so easily quantified and transmitted to students. Second, departments of sociology find too many of their students unprepared—and unmotivated—in mathematical and statistical skills. As a consequence, they must introduce special courses in mathematics, logic, and statistics before specialized techniques can be mastered. Third—and as a result of the second—too many methodological specialists have to spend their time communicating basic applied statistical knowledge to students and colleagues. Thus these specialists are too often distracted from more important problems of devising and applying more nearly adequate procedures for measurement and analysis.

## COMPARATIVE STUDY OF SOCIETIES

Men have never been neutral about the differences between themselves and neighboring clans, tribes, states, and nations. Sometimes these differences have been occasions for curiosity, sometimes for bellicosity. And while travelers and historians have throughout the ages recorded these differences, only since the rise of anthropology and sociology as social sciences have cultural differences become the subject of dispassionate scientific description and explanation.

In the past few decades, the comparative study of societies has shown great vitality. This has resulted partly from independent though somewhat simultaneous developments in anthropology, sociology, political science, and history. A great part of the impetus has come, too, from dissolution of colonial empires, emergence of former colonies as "new nations," and attempts of these nations to introduce rapid economic and social changes. These dynamic countries have come to command the attention of social scientists, and to demand comparative understanding of the changes they are experiencing.

### Traditions of Research

At least three separate intellectual traditions flow into the systematic comparative study of societies. The first, a very loose tradition, crystalized among the evolutionary anthropologists of the late nineteenth century—people like Sir James George Frazer (1854–1941), Sir Edward Burnett Tylor (1832–1917), and Lewis Henry Morgan (1818–81). These thinkers were mainly interested in ordering various societies on a scale from primitive to advanced, and describing the different technological, familial, political, and other institutional patterns at each stage of evolution. Their interest was mainly to reconstruct evolutionary history through detailed description of customs and institutions. By and large,

their concern with the reliability of data was casual, and their methodological sophistication was not great.

Some of the classical sociological thinkers made extensive use of comparative data on different groups and nations to draw inferences and
explain the differences. Max Weber's monumental attempt to show why
some religious systems are more conducive to rational economic activity
than others—in which he compared the great Western, Indian, and
Chinese civilizations—still stands as a landmark of systematic comparative illustration. Émile Durkheim also made systematic use of comparative data to strengthen his conclusions about the effects of social integration on behavior. For example, one of the central findings in his famous
study of suicide was that Protestants persistently experience higher rates
of suicide than Catholics. He explained this finding in terms of the different types of social integration of the two religious groupings: Protestants, with their anti-authoritarian, individualistic traditions are less
socially integrated than Catholics and hence less protected against self-
destruction. On examining the countries on which he had religious data,
however, Durkheim noticed that the Catholics were in the minority in
every case. Could it be, he asked, that social integration resulting from
minority status rather than religious tradition lies behind the lower
suicide rate of Catholics? To throw light on this question, he examined
Austria and Bavaria, where Catholics are in the majority. In these regions
he discovered somewhat smaller differences between Protestants and
Catholics in suicide rates, but the Protestant rates were still higher. On
the basis of these differences, Durkheim concluded that "Catholicism
does not owe [its protective influence] solely to its minority status." In
this operation Durkheim used neither experimental nor statistical techniques. Yet he was able to strengthen his inferences by the systematic
comparative illustration of national differences.

This tradition of explaining national differences through systematic
institutional description has continued to the present time, and many
of the accounts of the different experiences of the developing nations
fall within this tradition. Two modern examples of comparative institutional analysis are the work of Marion Levy, Jr., and Barrington Moore,
Jr. Levy traced the differences in speed of modernization in China and
Japan to distinctive family, stratification, and other institutional patterns. Moore sought to explain the divergent political histories of Britain,

Russia, Germany, and China in terms of the power relations among the major social classes in these countries. Many studies in this broad tradition use statistics when they are available; but often they have to rely on qualitative, institutional, and historical descriptions.

The second tradition, with its main roots in anthropology, goes under the name "cross-cultural analysis." This approach usually involves cross-sectional comparison of relatively large numbers of different cultures, using mainly descriptive ethnographic data. The typical procedure is to cross-tabulate different kinds of social characteristics to uncover generalizations about "what goes with what" in societies under various conditions. An example is Beatrice Whiting's cross-cultural study of fifty societies, in which she attempted to show that societies with systems of retaliatory justice against murder rely on sorcery as a cultural explanation of disease, whereas societies with systems of delegated authority to punish murderers do not rely on this explanation.

The major source of data for cross-cultural analysis is the Human Relations Area Files, designed originally at Yale in the 1930's as a device for ordering ethnographic materials to facilitate their use as a reference source on societies and their ready retrieval for comparative purposes. At present the Files embody materials on some 220 different cultures, described according to common categories. About ten years ago the Files, after many years of building, finally reached the point where they contained sufficient material for large-scale comparative use. Within recent years, enough comparative studies have accumulated to create a kind of "snowball effect" in cross-cultural comparative work. Investigators are able to take codes from the Files and combine them with their own data, thus expanding the scope of results quickly and inexpensively. The most ambitious compilation based on the Files to date is Robert Textor's A *Cross-Cultural Summary*, published in 1968. Because so much time and investment have gone into building this reservoir of data, an unusual situation for the social sciences has arisen: The payoff potential for cross-cultural analysis is increasing rapidly while the cost of research is declining precipitously because the facilities are already developed. It seems curious, therefore, that not many scholars have been working on cross-cultural analysis, and not much support has been forthcoming for these studies.

The third tradition of research has been labeled "cross-national analysis." While this tradition is not limited to any one discipline, it has been applied most by political scientists interested in comparing survey data on political attitudes and behavior in various countries. As the name implies, cross-national analysis involves comparisons of "nations" in the modern sense of the term; and, unlike many other forms of comparative analysis, it also usually involves the use of quantitative survey data or aggregated behavioral indices.

Cross-national analysis appears to be moving in the direction of establishing itself on an international basis. At the outset, numbers of scholars independently began developing archives of political data in various locations around the United States. This was followed by the establishment of an inter-university consortium for the exchange and standardization of data. Finally, the International Social Science Council has made some efforts to coordinate the building of archives in different countries. Some individual comparative studies—such as *The Civic Culture*, by Gabriel L. Almond and Sidney Verba—have relied on international cooperation in the collection of theoretically relevant data. We believe that this movement toward international cooperation in collecting data and building archives should receive maximum support. It promises to facilitate the exchange of comparable data, the coordination of field work, and the development of an international system of data gathered within a common theoretical framework. The utility of these international archives for the comparative study of societies can scarcely be exaggerated.

## Problems and Needs

A number of problems for comparative studies are posed by the current state of these three traditions of research. One of the main problems is that the traditions are far too independent of one another. Students of comparative institutional analysis are, in general, unaware of and sometimes unconcerned with the problems of methodology and research design that have occupied the attention of cross-cultural and cross-national investigators. Scholars making use of the Human Relations Area Files have not, in general, been interested in industrializing or industrialized countries, or in incorporating aggregated quantitative data into their studies. And finally, cross-national investigators have shown little interest in investigating ways in which cross-cultural research might help to establish general theoretical and conceptual bases for their own studies. Each group has much to learn from the others, and the mutual exchange of theoretical perspectives and research techniques would broaden the horizons of each and work toward the synthesis that is so evidently needed in the area of comparative studies.

Another major problem, related to the first, relates to the need to achieve a better integration among field research, the creation of archives, and theoretical analysis of comparative materials. Optimally, theoretical analysis should be based on archives produced by field research, and, in its turn, should inform field workers and archivists of better criteria of relevance for gathering and storing data. As matters stand, however, these several kinds of activity are often regarded as competitors rather than collaborators in the drive toward adequate scientific work; and too little effort is being expended to maximize the articulation among them. As a result, each type of activity is likely to become an enterprise in itself, conducted with little relation to the guidelines suggested by the others. At the very minimum, the promotion of comparative research requires recognition that all three activities are legitimate objects of scientific interest, that they must be systematically related to one another if scientific knowledge is to grow, and that their interconnections should be expedited rather than left to chance.

## DEMOGRAPHY

### The Field and Its Growth

Professional demographers ask many of the same questions asked by people who are interested in more practical matters of policy. What is happening to the size of the population in the world as a whole, in world regions, in nations, in provinces, and in localities? What combinations of causes are responsible for population growth or decline in these units? Why do some populations grow rapidly and others more slowly? Why does one society grow at one time, decline at another? Does our knowledge of the causes of growth provide us with means to predict the future? How do changes in the composition of a population—especially age, sex, and marital composition—affect its total rate of change? And, conversely, how does total growth affect a population's composition? How are changes in a population's growth and composition related to its spatial distribution?

Each of these questions may be approached from two points of view. *Formally*, a demographer attempts to break down population changes into processes occurring in different parts of the population. For example, he may wish to explain changes in fertility among successive cohorts of women by asking the rate at which women marry and the rate at which they bear children at different ages. *Substantively*, he attempts to explain these processes by referring to their social, economic, political, biological, and physical causes. To refer to the same example, he may wish to explain differences in women's rates of marriage by pointing to the society's distinctive cultural values, or economic structure, or perhaps to the psychological characteristics of the women involved. Formal demography tends to be relatively neat because it is essentially a system of accounting for a phenomenon by breaking it down into component parts; substantive demography is less so, because it encounters a multiplicity of interacting variables, the relations among which are only dimly understood.

Although demography necessarily cuts across many disciplines, many demographers are sociologists, and the results of demographic research are useful for many sociological purposes. Most research on population is done in departments of sociology, though some also occurs in the other social science departments, and in biomedical disciplines, such as population genetics and public health. A few universities have recently created separate departments of demography. In the United States, more than elsewhere, departments of sociology offer most of the formal undergraduate and graduate training in demography, though schools of public health have become more active at the graduate level.

Since World War II demography has grown very rapidly. The Population Association of America has grown from 500 to 1,500 members—half of whom are sociologists—in the past decade. The membership of the International Union for the Scientific Study of Population—one fifth of which is American—has more than doubled in the same period. The annual number of entries in *Population Index*, the standard bibliographic source, rose from about 2,000 in 1950 to nearly 5,000 in 1965, despite stricter standards of inclusion. Many institutes for research and training flourish in the United States; most of them did not exist ten years ago.

The main impetus for the growth has been the increasing awareness of the policy implications of demographic knowledge. Only a short time ago few were aware of population problems, and few were interested in or willing to discuss family planning; now, "the population explosion" and "birth control" are household words. Lyndon Johnson was the first President to outline a clear official position on population policy at home and abroad. Part of the increased awareness of population problems, it should be noted, rests on improvements in demographic knowledge, and increased understanding of the ramification of population changes throughout the fabric of society. We shall indicate a few of the major strands in the history of demographic analysis.

## Historical Trends

Demographic inquiry has a long history. In the seventeenth and eighteenth centuries, when population size was thought to contribute to the growth and strength of nations, it was known as "political arithmetic." In the nineteenth century the focus shifted, largely because of the theories of Thomas Robert Malthus (1766–1834), to the negative economic effects of a large population. The development of demography as an empirical science was assisted greatly when countries began establishing registration and census systems. Indeed, in the United States demography and democracy went hand in hand; the first regular decennial census in 1790 was introduced as a basis for calculating political representation.

Because demographers have always been preoccupied with population growth, they have also been interested in its mechanisms and processes. The first impressive accomplishment of classical mathematical demography was the demonstration that in the developed countries a population might be growing yet at the same time be destined for decline if vital behavior remained the same. The mechanism responsible for this apparent paradox lay in the relations between a population's birth and death rates. For instance, if a population was experiencing a rapid decline in death rates, it could be increasing substantially, even if birth rates were also declining. If this situation persisted, however, the age composition of the population would gradually alter, with the result that a smaller proportion of the women would be of child-bearing age, and the natural increase of population would gradually change to a natural decrease. Extending this important principle of the relation between fertility and mortality, the classical demographers were able to devise a variety of population projections by making different assumptions about the behavior of each component of change.

More recently demographers have demonstrated that fertility rates in developed countries decline at different rates among different parts of the population. Early in the century it was discovered that people at higher socio-economic levels had lower fertility rates than those below them, and that urban residents had lower rates than rural residents. These facts suggested to many that the reproductive vigor and the population in advanced countries were on the decline. Subsequent investigations indicate, however, that these earlier relations between socio-economic structure and fertility were probably transitory, and that as methods of regulating birth diffuse throughout the population, the relations may disappear or even be reversed.

On the basis of these kinds of discoveries, demographers constructed the famous "model of demographic transition." According to this model, population changes proceeded by several stages:

*Stage 1:* High death rates and equally high birth rates. Resultant rate of population growth: zero.

*Stage 2:* Decline of death rates but not of birth rates. Resultant rate of growth: positive and increasing.

*Stage 3:* Continued decline of death rates and decline of birth rates. Resultant rate of growth: positive but no longer increasing.

*Stage 4:* Low death rates and equally low birth rates. Resultant rate of growth: diminishing toward zero.

To explain this sequence, demographers argued that death rates declined early because of improvements in public health associated with social and economic advances, but that birth rates declined only after people began to realize that children were a cost without an economic

advantage in an urban-industrial society. And the longer this lag between changes in the birth and death rates, they argued further, the
greater the growth of population.

This simplified model has been refined by considering it in terms of
the behavior of cohorts rather than of the movements of conventional
death and birth rates. The accompanying graphs illustrate this refinement. In Figure 2-1a, an assumed lag between declining death rates and
declining birth rates is represented in terms of the rates assumed for
different cohorts born in successive years. When this experience of
cohorts is translated into crude death and birth rates (Figure 2-1b), a
much more pronounced lag is produced. This results in turn in a much
greater natural increase than that experienced by the cohorts themselves
(Figure 2-1c) and a dramatic multiplication of the size of the population
(Figure 2-1d). One important implication of this refined model is that
the greatest growth of population caused by the transition occurs long
after the transition itself begins. In the model illustrated in the graphs,
for example, crude death rates fall to their terminal level during the

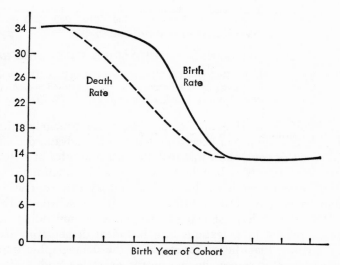

FIGURE 2-1a    TRANSITION MODEL: ASSUMED EXPERIENCE OF
COHORTS

first hundred years of the transition period (Figure 2-1b), but population multiplies eight times subsequently (Figure 2-1d).

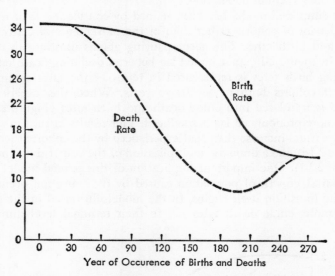

**FIGURE 2-1b    TRANSLATION INTO CRUDE PERIOD VITAL RATES**

Source: N. B. Ryder, "The Translation Model of Demographic Change," in *Emerging Techniques of Population Research* (New York: Milbank Memorial Fund, 1963), pp. 71, 76, 78, 79.

Before World War II many demographers had concluded that the demographic transition had been completed in the advanced countries. The basis for this conclusion was that the intrinsic rates of natural increase in these countries had fallen to low and sometimes negative levels. Subsequent experience has indicated that this conclusion was premature; most advanced countries have grown substantially since World War II and have shown no symptoms of impending decline. Increasingly refined investigations into historical demography have revealed, moreover, that the earlier stages of the demographic transition were, like the later stages, by no means as stable and uniform as postulated in the original model.

In the recent history of the developing countries, the beginnings of

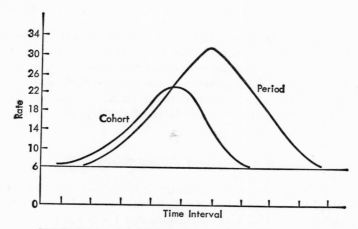

**FIGURE 2-1c    RATES OF NATURAL INCREASE**

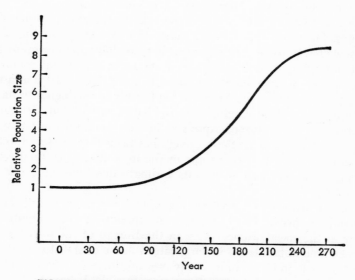

**FIGURE 2-1d    RELATIVE POPULATION SIZE OVER TIME**

development witnessed, as in the West, declining mortality and persistently high fertility. But the pace of mortality decline has been much faster than it was in the older industrial countries—so fast, in fact, that many demographers are apprehensive that the new, developing countries are in danger of being caught in a vicious circle of unprecedented population growth that prevents the level of development necessary for fertility to decline.

## Current Trends and Future Needs

These kinds of dramatic demographic phenomena have underscored the needs for better population data and for better methodology and theory. The United Nations has taken some major strides toward improving the collection of data by systematically compiling national population statistics and standardizing the procedures for producing these statistics in many nations. Sample surveys have been used to estimate demographic data where registration and census figures are defective or nonexistent. These surveys, moreover, can be used to yield deeper and more detailed information than is available in some official statistics. On the basis of several series of such surveys in the United States, we have learned, for instance, that the differential levels of fertility in the different socio-economic strata are probably not so much a result of more or fewer children desired in the different strata as a result of the greater effectiveness in regulating fertility in the higher strata. Surveys in some of the developing countries have revealed that, despite high fertility rates, many citizens express an interest in family limitation. One reason for the success of these surveys has been that, despite initial expectations to the contrary, people in the most diverse cultural settings are not at all reluctant to discuss intimate questions in confidential interviews.

As in so many other sciences, the digital computer is transforming demographic theory. The first large-scale applications of computer technology in the social sciences were in the Bureau of the Census, which has been able to tabulate a much greater volume of statistics in the past twenty years than it had in its entire previous history. The computer has made refined population projections more feasible. It has also facilitated the application of quasi-stable population theory, by which the probable values for an array of demographic parameters are inferred from only a few benchmark data when adequate statistics are not available. Using this theory, demographers have developed knowledge about the relations between changes in vital rates and changes in the age distribution of a population. For example, we have learned that the long-run decline in the birth rate (not the tendency for people to live longer, as common sense would suggest) is the principal cause of increasing proportions of old people in advanced countries. Finally, the computer has been used to apply stochastic models to the study of the interacting influences of the level of fecundity, efficacy of contraception, and frequency of fetal mortality on eventual family size.

All these developments clearly require more support for demographic research and better training programs. Future demographers must have greater competence in mathematics and more experience in manipulating complex data. Within a few years, any up-to-date center of research and training in population will require access to banks of machine-readable data drawn both from official statistics throughout the world and from surveys designed for testing and evaluation. Trainees will have to learn to manipulate these data, and to program elaborate calculations on many types of demographic models.

Although future demographers will analyze official statistics more intensively than now, this type of analysis will diminish in proportion to all demographic research. We may expect a vast increase in the use of detailed surveys. If demographers are to trace trends in family size and estimate their impact on future population growth, they will have to conduct frequent and detailed surveys on reproductive histories, contraceptive practices, preferences and expectations about family size, as well as research on social and economic conditions affecting family size. The study of social and geographic mobility will also call for substantial enterprises in collecting data. As the relations between demographic factors and socio-economic processes come to be better understood, demographers will be forced to broaden their research well beyond the classical problems of formal demography.

In the immediate future, the policy implications of demography will continue to concern problems posed by sheer numbers of people, changes in these numbers, and changes in the rates of change. Looking toward the long run, however, it is possible to forecast that demographic research—on patterns of social mobility, for example—will have direct relevance for the policy-maker's concern with the distribution of the abundance of society, and his concern with the conditions that maximize human equality.

## SOCIAL STRATIFICATION

Social stratification involves the study of how the good things of life are distributed in society—good things such as wealth, power, prestige, information and skill, legal immunities and privileges, and informal social advantages such as contacts with important people. It also involves the study of who has access to these things, and why. Finally, it includes the study of how the differential distribution of status and rewards affects people's attitudes, behavior, patterns of inter-action, and group memberships.

Within this area of interest, students of social stratification are likely to ask the following kinds of questions. How great are inequalities in wealth, power, prestige, and the rest of the good things of life, in different historical periods and in different parts of the world? Are different kinds of inequality matched or mismatched in any given society—that is to say, are the rich at the same time powerful and prestigious, or are there discrepancies in the distribution of these several rewards? (This is the problem of "status consistency," as it has been termed by sociologists.) What determines where an individual becomes situated on the various status scales—his own motivation, attitudes and behavior; his family, community, or ethnic background; or the structure of social opportunities and obstacles? What factors determine whether a person is able to move from one status position to another in his lifetime? What is the impact of social status on family structure, child-rearing, political behavior, and consumer behavior? Are some types of stratification systems more conducive to democratic political structure than others? To what degree do stratification systems engender social conflict and social change?

Needless to say, stratification touches almost all other areas of sociological inquiry. Much comparative historical sociology has stressed problems of class structure and its changes, and much demographic research has elucidated the conditions and consequences of stratification. As a matter of fact, social stratification turns out to be empirically associated with thousands of different attributes and types of behavior—the incidence of mental illness, political attitudes and voting behavior, class consciousness, criminal activity, divorce, drinking patterns, and attendance at movies and baseball games, to name but a few. To summarize the field of stratification, then, would be to summarize much of sociology. The observations that follow, therefore, are necessarily highly selective.

## Theoretical Analysis

In the study of stratification, as in many other branches of sociology, it is possible to identify a tradition of developing theory and a tradition of accumulating empirical knowledge. Unfortunately, the relationship between the two is not always as close as is scientifically desirable. Sometimes theories of stratification call definite empirical data into question, but not always; sometimes empirical studies of stratification and its correlates are related to some body of theory, but not often enough. We anticipate that, as the field continues to advance, the two types of activity will become more closely wedded than they are at present.

Theories of stratification are diverse in content and emphasis. Karl Marx and C. Wright Mills emphasized the importance of "objective" factors such as economic and political control as determinants of stratification. Thorstein Veblen and W. Lloyd Warner stressed more subjective determinants such as personal reputation. Max Weber viewed society as consisting of separate hierarchies based on wealth, power, and prestige, and traced the implications of discrepancies among these hierarchies. Talcott Parsons and Kingsley Davis developed theories of stratification that fall within an organic model of society associated with the tradition of functional analysis.

The theoretical side of the study of stratification has always been burdened by ideological controversy, much of which traces back several centuries. In the eighteenth and nineteenth centuries, as the aristocracy was declining and as the middle and working classes were rising in western Europe, conservatives and radicals established two sharply di-

verging intellectual traditions. Conservatives were alarmed by the decline of the social order based on legally fixed status categories; as a
result they insisted on the preservation of status inequalities to maintain
social order. Radicals also saw the same decline, but they concluded
that it had not gone far enough; as a result they insisted on eradication
of the surviving inequalities of the old order, which they saw as the
basis of social exploitation and injustice. These two traditions are still
very much alive in theoretical debates, although their guise has changed.
One contemporary school of thought in stratification theory stresses the
ordering and integrating aspects of stratification systems, and harks back
to the conservative position; the other stresses the exploitative and con-
flict-producing aspects, and is reminiscent of the radical tradition. Obviously any complete theory of stratification must involve a synthesis
of both aspects.

## Empirical Research

        The accumulation of sociological knowledge on social strat-
ification has been impressive, but it has also been irregular. At the risk of
oversimplifying, we point out that sociologists have been more effective in
measuring and analyzing prestige than they have been in measuring and
analyzing the ranking of power, wealth, and prerogatives. Consider only
two examples. First, sociologists studying stratification have produced a
number of reliable findings on the apparently refractory topic of occupational prestige. As indicated by our earlier discussion of comparative
stratification, hierarchies of prestige have been discovered to be surprisingly invariant from society to society. In addition, patterns of correlation between occupational prestige and phenomena such as spending patterns, leisure activities, and political preferences have been both
discovered and replicated. The emergence of such findings relates in part
to the fact that sociologists have devised measures of occupational prestige that are applicable from society to society, using the survey method.
By contrast, many of the sociologists of power relations, focusing mainly
on local communities, have conducted extensive debates and experimentation with alternative methods of research. They have not yet, however,
produced a scientifically usable criterion for the measurement of power
hierarchies. Second, sociologists of stratification have conducted a suc-

cession of increasingly sophisticated studies of social mobility, and have uncovered revealing and theoretically provocative evidence on the invariance of historical and comparative rates of mobility. By contrast, studies of the influence of social stratification on political participation, collective behavior, and social movements have generated provocative hypotheses and conjectures, but have been less impressive in accumulating reliable findings.

How can we account for these contrasts? One explanation is surely the difference in the respective methods of research. For both pairs of contrasts, the more highly developed area of research was able to adapt the technique of population surveys to the collection and analysis of data. Both census data and extensive sample surveys have produced a wealth of data on occupational stratification and its correlates. The adaptation of the survey technique to the study of power and politics, however, is relatively underdeveloped, except for the survey of political preferences and the study of voting statistics.

Another factor is a difference in conceptual refinement. Even though many sociologists have been keenly interested in the phenomenon of "power" in recent years, they have not been able to produce theoretically fruitful statements about how power operates in stratification systems. Formulations such as "the power structure" and "the establishment," often borrowed from ideological discourse, have not proven sufficiently precise to make the necessary conceptual discriminations. Clearly it is essential to distinguish between what gives rise to power and what determines who is to enjoy it. And from the standpoint of the analysis of stratification, it is necessary to account for differential access to positions of power, and thus to disclose how the holding of power is related to other forms of social status.

## The Future of Research on Stratification

How is progress to be most effectively encouraged in those areas of stratification that have lagged? One obvious strategy is to expand the basic research support available to sociologists and political scientists who are striving to produce and refine more sensitive conceptual formulations. On the side of the collection and analysis of data, it is essential to strive toward two closely related objectives—to make statistics gathered more theoretically relevant to sociological analysis, and to extend the technique of the national survey to include topics hitherto covered only sporadically and locally.

With respect to the first objective, it is frustrating to the sociologist that so few of the vast quantity of federal statistics are tabulated and analyzed in a way that bears on theoretically important issues. Consider the recent analysis of the characteristics of very wealthy persons in the United States by economists employed by the Board of Governors of the Federal Reserve System. The study was based on sampling defined by current income, and was made feasible because the economists had access to individual records of the government's detailed income surveys. This study is very informative about the sources of wealth and some of the correlations between wealth and other social-status categories. But the data are of little use to sociologists because they contain no information on the roles of the wealthy in society, their social origins, their patterns of interaction, and their personal values and attitudes. Until comparable data on these and other relevant sociological variables become available, the sociological—as distinguished from the economic—aspects of wealth will remain matters of ignorance or ill-informed speculation.

Second, because the official statistical system does not include indicators of many of the apparently crucial sociological variables, the investigator must too often rely on small, local, or poorly designed samples. For example, one of the important preoccupations of investigators of social mobility is determination of the respective impact on status achievement of (a) mental ability, (b) aspiration and ambition, and (c) circumstances of social origin. Yet there has never been an adequate national sample that systematically measures and combines these variables. A properly designed study would require reliable measurement of a number of such variables, and would be applied periodically on a substantial sample of persons over a period of years. Such a study design has been approximated by Project TALENT, and much important information on status achievement may be expected from it. But even this project falls short of a design that would be desirable for sociological research.

Many topics in social stratification touch matters of social policy and social reform very closely. Much of the sociologist's research on stratification has been relevant to the emerging labor movement and industrial conflict in past decades. More recently, sociological research on stratification has become applicable to problems of poverty, welfare, and opportunities for the underprivileged. As it happens, some of the most extensive work on stratification has concerned the distribution of "opportunity" in American society, as in investigations of the relationship between social origin and ultimate status achievement. It has been demonstrated, for example, that the educational system is moderately successful in opening up possibilities for social mobility for children of modest background who have high motivation and better-than-average mental ability. Less expected, however, has been the finding that American society has not been becoming more "rigid" or "closed," and indeed that, if anything, opportunities for mobility are more widely distributed than they were several decades ago. Such findings clearly do not deny that the restriction of opportunity—especially that based on race—is still too high to be compatible with the basic American value of equality of opportunity. But they permit us to approach the policy problems involved in maximizing opportunities for social mobility in a more informed and selective manner than was possible in the past.

## COMPLEX ORGANIZATIONS

Modern society is, perhaps more than anything else, an organizational society. While the ancient empires and medieval civilization generated political, religious, and military bureaucracies, it remained for industrial and post-industrial Western civilization to produce a profusion of large-scale, complex administrative organizations that pervade many aspects of social life. Complex organizations today dominate not only business, industry, government, and the military, but have been extended to education, research, the mass media, labor, recreation, and voluntary philanthropy. And it is safe to predict that America in the year 2,000 will be even more an organizational society than it is today.

### Major Approaches to the Study of Organizations

The central place of large-scale organization in industrial society was, however, far from obvious to the early observers of the Industrial Revolution, such as the classical economists and Karl Marx. The sociological pioneer in the analysis of complex organizations was Max Weber. Weber stressed above all that bureaucracy, in contrast to traditional and spontaneously generated organizations, is an *efficient* type of organization. (Common sense and popular folklore emphasize its sluggishness and red tape.) He defined the complex organization as a structure of purposive activities directed toward the achievement of explicit objectives, such as profit-making. The complex organization, as characterized by Weber, assumes adequately motivated personnel. In addition, it presumes certain organizational objectives that are already established, and adequate means for attaining these objectives. To maximize its efficiency, Weber argued, a complex administrative organization develops a system of highly specialized jobs, a set of systematic rules and procedures, a pyramid of authority, an emphasis on "the position" rather than "the person" as the important unit of organization, and the principle of distributing rewards according to position and performance. According to this view of bureaucracy, efficiency can be maximized by rearranging jobs and altering rules, and administration is thereby freed from the potential inefficiencies of nepotism and personal loyalties, traditional rules of thumb, and subversion of organizational objectives. For a long period of time in the early twentieth century Weber's somewhat bloodless view of bureaucracy dominated organizational research, and, on the applied level, was echoed in the American "scientific management" movement associated with the name of Frederick W. Taylor.

A number of different approaches to complex organization have been developed in the various social and behavioral sciences. Economists and students of business administration have initiated new developments in the theory of the firm; historians have traced bureaucratic forms to their most informal beginnings; political scientists have taken up the study of systems of public administration and civil service; psychologists have developed an interest in industrial morale and other psychological aspects of complex organizations; and sociologists have continued their study of role specialization, the structure of authority, and patterns of communication and interaction. As these streams of research emerged and raised new issues, it became apparent that the two central assumptions of Weber's classical model—that personnel are adequately motivated and that organizational objectives are fixed and known—do not always apply. Accordingly, many advances in research have been made by modifying or dropping one or both of these assumptions. In fact, the several dominant sociological approaches to the study of formal organization can be grouped conveniently according to their positions on these assumptions in the following way:

|  | **Organizational objectives assumed to be "given"** | **Organizational objectives assumed to be problematical** |
|---|---|---|
| Motivation of personnel assumed to be "given" | "Classical" approach | "Decision-making" approach |
| Motivation of personnel assumed to be problematical | "Human relations" approach | "Natural systems" approach |

We have already outlined the essentials of the classical approach. The "human relations" approach, associated with the names of Elton Mayo and Fritz J. Roethlisberger, views the organization as a group of people with varying degrees of motivation and commitment to formal organizational activities. Research in this tradition has revealed that close and authoritarian supervision or repetitive technological demands are likely to undermine morale and generate dissatisfaction among workers, and lead to absenteeism, high turnover, and quiet subversion of productive efficiency. Informal groups in formal organizations have also been discovered to be a very powerful medium for crystalizing employees' attitudes, and translating them into forces that either expedite or interfere with organizational objectives. The human relations approach has demonstrated that people are not simply another part of the technological apparatus of an organization, and if managers attempt to treat them that way, their policies might well backfire and engender dissatisfactions and inefficiencies. Accordingly, investigators in this tradition have emphasized the importance of meaningful social relationships in the work place, and the importance of sympathetic recognition of employees' social and psychological needs by employers. Their emphasis has been criticized, however—mainly by those sympathetic with the interests of the working man—for neglecting genuine conflicts of interest between management and workers by over-stressing good communication, and for providing management with techniques for manipulating workers psychologically.

The "decision-making" approach treats the decisions about organizational objectives and how to achieve them as a major problem to be solved, rather than one that has been solved. In their most rigorous form, models of organizational decision-making focus on the flow of information and communication, and seek to specify optimal strategies for reaching decisions when information is not complete. Sociologists have made use of this approach rather less than economists and students of business administration, largely because it deals with impersonal processes, rather than people in distinctive social roles.

The "natural systems" approach assumes neither a set of fixed objectives nor adequate motivation. Organizational processes are viewed naturalistically, related to developing interaction patterns among people with different ideas and outlooks. This approach has the merit of analyzing interpersonal and intergroup conflicts as they develop rather than assuming that they do not arise or that they are automatically solved. Indeed, the organization often appears to be a partisan political system rather than a bureaucracy, according to some accounts. Yet for all its realism, the "natural systems" approach is inhibited theoretically because it does not proceed within a systematic set of limiting assumptions, as the other approaches do. Thus it is better at generating case descriptions than at formulating general principles.

## Needs for Theory and Research

Each of these approaches—with the exception of the "natural systems" approach—has been molded into a more or less coherent theoretical statement. It is evident that none of the theories is either "right" or "wrong" in any absolute sense. Each one taps one or more aspects of organizational processes, and each carries forth its analysis on the basis of its own definite assumptions. In addition, each can properly be criticized for neglecting one or another important aspect of complex organizations. And while a theoretical synthesis among the several approaches is certainly possible in principle, sociologists have found it difficult up to now to combine these approaches into an integrated whole. In fact, the central problem to be faced by organization theory in the coming years is to determine how these several aspects of social organization can be synthesized into a coherent theoretical system. This problem will become all the more challenging as technology continues to increase in complexity, as the structure of organizations continues to become even more labyrinthine, and as the tentacles of complex organization continue to reach out in more and more directions.

To attack this problem effectively, sociologists must both open new theoretical vistas and collect and analyze new types of data. Too much sociological theory and research has been based mainly on the model of a single organization, and attention has been focused on its internal processes, by and large. Surely this dominant model is not sufficient to analyze newer and more complex organizational forms such as the interlocking networks of organization in the civil service, the multi-campus state university, regional consortia of educational institutions, multioutlet distributive organizations in business, and multi-plant industrial concerns. Having become rooted in its social and technological environment and more complex ways, organizations find themselves both constraining and being constrained by these environments in new ways. Yet investigators of formal organizations have barely begun to attack these new relationships. Their attention must be directed to organizations within organizations, and the relations among organizational systems. Since automation and other applications of the computer are changing working conditions radically—while challenging some of our cherished generalizations about the effects of the work place on people, as in the case of worker alienation discussed above—it will be essential for sociologists continuously to seek for principles under which to incorporate both the old and the new findings.

These new needs call for new and improved methods and techniques of empirical research. Until recently, the main type of investigation has been the case study of an individual organization, into which the investigator has absorbed himself in some way—as interviewer or participant observer, for example—and has written up his results within some kind of theoretical framework. In the past few years, however, sociological investigators have increasingly felt the need to study *large numbers of organizations on a systematic and comparative basis* to increase the reliability, validity, and representativeness of results. This trend toward analysis of aggregated numbers of organizations must continue if knowledge is to increase. Cross-national studies of complex organizations are also matters of high priority, particularly since the developing nations are all forging new types of political, economic, and social organizations as they attempt to enter the modern world. Systematic comparisons among these nations, as well as comparisons with the historical development of complex organizations of the West, would contribute greatly to our knowledge of the dynamics of organizational change. In connection with the study of dynamics, sociologists could also profit from a series of systematic longitudinal studies of organizations over periods of several years, to supplement the largely cross-sectional research that has dominated the field up to now.

One of the perennial problems that has hindered the investigation of complex organizations has been that of gaining access to organizations for study, and—once that is gained—of gaining access to information within organizations. Even under the most ideal circumstances, research in an organization is likely to interfere with the work of busy people and possibly disrupt its operations. In addition, all organizations have well-guarded secrets, functionaries who do not want people prying, and cliques that keep to themselves; and there is no reason why organizational personnel would want to open up to sociological investigators any more than they open up to one another. Students of complex organizations must turn their ingenuity to a number of interrelated issues connected with the problem of difficult access. They must seek new ways of gaining the confidence of organizational personnel, while at the same time remaining sensitive to the ethical problems of privacy and organizational autonomy. They must be scrupulous in representing their research interests straightforwardly, preserving the anonymity of their informants, and reporting their data accurately, so that they will continue to merit the confidence of those they study. When first-hand data are not available for one reason or another, they must be more inventive in drawing inferences from those data that are public knowledge. In short, sociologists studying complex organizations, as well as other topics, should be encouraged both to discover new ways of gaining data and to sharpen their interpretative tools when inevitable gaps in their data become evident.

### SOCIALIZATION

Most sociologists believe that their discipline should focus on the study of groups and social structures. Up to a point these can be studied in their own right, without reference to the people who constitute them—but only up to a point. For example, a sociologist can legitimately and profitably study the relationship between types of social stratification systems and types of family structure. But sooner or later he has to know something about the people involved. A system of social stratification will operate only as long as people value and seek the prestige, power, and other rewards it offers; and a family system will not persist without a measure of personal loyalty and affection among family members. Thus sociologists cannot leave the individual entirely to other disciplines.

*Socialization* is a prime example of a phenomenon that demands both sociological and psychological knowledge. Defined simply, socialization encompasses those processes by which an individual learns to take account of the social order, and to cope with it by some combination of conformity, nonconformity, avoidance, and conflict. (This sociological definition should not be confused with the politico-economic definition, which refers to the nationalization of industry.) This definition necessarily looks toward both the social order and the individual. Thus, it is essential that scholars in each discipline heed the theory and research of the other in studying socialization. Consider, for example, the study of how conscience develops in a child—a common topic for a student of socialization. The investigator must know something both about the character of social norms and about psychological principles of learning, identification, and personality formation. If he relies on uninformed assumptions about either, his research will suffer accordingly. A special argument can therefore be made for the need for collaboration between sociologists and psychologists in the study of socialization.

#### Research Trends

Research on socialization has moved in several directions during the past decade or two. One common preoccupation is the study of alienation from society, an example of which we presented in the work of Robert Blauner on worker dissatisfaction. In particular, sociologists have conducted much research on the hypothesis that modern industrial societies generate pervasive disaffection, which in turn gives rise to responses such as apathy, deviance, or organized protest activity. A related hypothesis is that in modern society a state of anomie (or normlessness) gives rise to an attitude of anomie (or passive despair) in many citizens. Leo Srole devised a scale for measuring anomie that has been used in many surveys to measure this attitude. Anomie has been found to be correlated both with socio-economic status and various personality characteristics, indicating once again that both social and psychological factors have a place in its genesis.

A second major development in the past two decades has been the study of the impact of family structure on personality formation. Psychiatrists and educators initiated this line of work as they sought connections between child-rearing techniques and specific behavioral consequences. Sociologists later joined in as the emphasis shifted away from child-rearing techniques toward the nature of family relationships. Substantively, sociologists have been interested in social-class differences in the exercise of authority in the family, the closeness of family bonds, and the division of responsibilities by sex. They have also conducted extensive research in many countries on the impact of education, religious values, and deferred gratification in the family on the achievement motive, which is thought to be an important psychological source of upward mobility.

A third important trend is the study of adult socialization. Because the adult can recognize and resist influences more than the child, and because he has a well-formed set of attitudes that he must give up if he is to replace it with new ones, adult socialization often undermines the established self. Recent work has depicted the critical transition from adolescence to independent and responsible adulthood. Sociologists have also studied the difficulties of intensive reorientation of the individual as he moves through institutions such as military colleges and professional schools. Studies of aging have focused on the personal readjustment that is imposed by the end of active parenthood for women and occupational retirement for men. Finally, sociologists have documented the drastic reorientations imposed by "total institutions," such as prisons and mental hospitals, and the difficulties of reorienting individuals who have been inmates toward outside life.

A fourth emphasis in recent research concerns the impact of group membership on attitudes and behavior—for example, the impact of neighborhood play groups on the child, or the impact of primary groups in adult settings like the army. Some studies conducted within the framework of "reference group theory" suggest that a person will adopt the values of a given group to the extent that the group is a cohesive one. More refined hypotheses take account of role differentiation within groups, and suggest, for example, that leaders tend to be more strongly committed than followers to group values, yet at the same time are accorded greater freedom to vary from strict adherence to group norms.

Finally, research on socialization has become increasingly comparative. Within the United States some sociologists have expressed concern that existing theories of socialization may apply only to middle-class American populations. Family patterns in Brazil have been used to test hypotheses concerning family determinants of the motivation to achieve. Studies of the acquisition of language have been replicated in several cultures.

## Problems and Needs

Sociologists have long been concerned with a number of persistent problems of measurement and conceptualization, which plague studies in socialization. Too little is known about relationships between attitudes and behavior. Studies that correlate one attitude measure with another are being viewed with increasing skepticism. Inventing "motives" or "attitudes" with simple one-to-one correspondence with some aspect of behavior is regarded as equally unhelpful. As sociologists continue their attack on these problems, two new emphases emerge. One is that the commonplace that the individual "constructs" reality as he attempts to come to terms with his social environment should be taken seriously. Ethnomethodologists and others are turning their attention to uncovering the unstated assumptions and rules that people share in situations of personal interaction, and the taken-for-granted ways in which they communicate these assumptions and rules to one another. A second emphasis is on dealing with attitudes and behavior in terms of their "fit" with social situations rather than as variables with their own inherent nature and dimensions. "Leadership behavior," for example, is not to be regarded as a thing in itself, but rather a relationship in which the behavior of one person is accepted as a conditional basis for following him. And the same may be true for personality variables that have long been thought to be fixed dispositions—such as authoritarianism, nurturance, and the tendency to conform.

Just as overly simple characterizations of attitudes and behavior will probably be replaced, more complex causal models will make their appearance in the coming years. Instead of inquiring into extremely general relationships—such as between mass society and alienation—sociologists will refine their questions. What specific *kinds* of experience in mass society causes alienation? In what *specific* situations will a minority-group member experience feelings of marginality or rejection? Interactive models—aided by modern computer technology—will also assume greater importance. These models can represent socialization as a continuous process: The child has an experience, which leads him to respond in a given way; his behavior evokes responses from others, which constitute experiences that evoke still other rounds of responses from the child and his social environment.

Research on socialization will also be affected by the crises of our times. What are the differences in perspective and motivation associated with the "cultures" of rebellion? How is an individual socialized into a "culture of poverty" in such a way that he seems unable to break out of it? How can these patterns of socialization be changed most effectively? What are the future needs for research on socialization likely to be? Most research in the past has been done on a microscopic level. To extend the applicability of findings and theories, it is necessary to establish adequate facilities for macroscopic and comparative research. The establishment of an international network of research centers on socialization would greatly improve the present arrangements for personal mastery of languages, special training, and coordination of research on an *ad hoc* basis.

The need for studies that trace subjects over a long period of time is great in many branches of sociology, but especially in the study of socialization, which, by definition, often takes a long time. Yet the obstacles to effective longitudinal studies are considerable. It is often difficult and expensive to locate the same individuals at several points in time; and it is often impracticable to secure data from subjects who have moved long distances from original sites of investigation. The first obstacle can be reduced by developing ways to use social security and other forms of public identification to trace individuals—without, of course, infringing on individual rights to privacy. The second can be reduced by establishing cooperative relations among research centers in various locations, or planning research on a national rather than a local scale. Even with improvements such as these, however, longitudinal studies will continue to be among the most difficult and expensive kinds of research.

Perhaps the most pressing need is to develop methods for experimental studies of socialization outside the laboratory—studies such as the field experiment on family planning in Taiwan. It is important to develop appraisal studies as accompaniments to such programs, and to involve the research team into the initial design and scheduling of the intervention, so that closer approximations to the experimental method can be achieved. As we have said, such experiments pose a number of delicate ethical issues. In actuality, however, every business organization that employs a new sales technique, every school that introduces a new teaching method, every publisher who markets a book on child-rearing techniques is intervening in some way in the lives of many people. The kind of sociological research we have in mind is systematic tracking and analysis of the kinds of intervention that occur in the lives of people who are undergoing any kind of socialization.

Because the study of socialization so often straddles many disciplines, it is essential to improve facilities—such as institutes, research centers, and laboratories—for interdisciplinary collaboration in teaching and research by sociologists, psychologists, anthropologists, and other scholars interested in socialization.

Finally, we note that the common practice of funding agencies to make grants only for specific projects works a particular hardship on studies of socialization. Usually these grants are for quite limited objectives and for restricted time periods. But the essence of socialization studies is to identify changes in attitudes and other personality variables that follow significant experiences and frequently take some time to become consolidated. With a programmatic instead of a project grant, the investigator could be flexible in his selection of an approach, use longitudinal rather than one-time research designs, and carry out supplemental studies to intensify the investigation of promising findings. Funding agencies might well expand such grants, which, with proper reviewing procedures, would provide much-needed flexibility to the study of socialization.

## DEVIANCE AND SOCIAL CONTROL

If American sociology could be said to be rooted historically in any single preoccupation, it would have to be the concern with social deviance and social problems. In the late nineteenth century and into the first few decades of the twentieth century, sociologists concentrated on such specific problems as crime, family disorganization, and the assimilation of immigrants, and on the ways and means of solving these problems. Many sociologists actually initiated or became involved in movements of social reform directed toward the amelioration of what were regarded as the social evils of the day.

As sociologists began their attempt to create a scientific discipline, many of the objectives of social reform were left to the emerging profession of social work. Nevertheless, many sociologists continued—and still continue—to describe and explain social problems such as crime, social dependency, prostitution, alcoholism, drug addiction, mental illness, divorce and unemployment. In the past two or three decades, however, they have come to study these phenomena in new and different ways. Instead of regarding each social problem as a separate object of study and possible change in its own right, sociologists have come more and more to study these problems within the context of general theories of deviance and social control.

Part of the impetus to study these problems in their general social context came from the theoretical writings of William I. Thomas, Pitirim Sorokin, Talcott Parsons, and Robert K. Merton. Another source, however, was the independent realization on the part of sociological investigators that no single social problem can be adequately understood without posing basic questions about the development and enforcement of rules, the conditions under which the legitimacy of rules is challenged, the development of subcultures that condone deviant behavior, and the impact of measures of social control on deviant behavior. Such questions invite comparative—rather than single-case—study of the situation of the delinquent, the mental patient, the hobo, the drug addict, and others who are defined as social deviants.

This trend toward more systematic treatment of deviance has evoked a renewed interest in social control. In previous generations, social control was treated primarily as everything that contributed to the maintenance of social order. It is now becoming plain, however, that the individual deviant, as well as the phenomenon of deviance in general, cannot be understood apart from society's efforts to prevent or correct deviant behavior. The career of the individual criminal is shaped as much by how others react to his behavior as it is by his personal motivations; the career of a social protest movement is shaped as much by the reactions of public authorities as it is by the characteristics of its participants; and, as has become painfully evident to most Americans in the past ten years, the understanding of individual and social violence cannot be separated from social efforts to control the use of weapons and deal with potential and actual offenders. Because of this new awareness, sociologists are beginning to study reactions to deviance as an integral part of deviance itself.

Finally, sociologists have become much more interested in collective forms of deviance than they were in the past. The pioneering studies of F. M. Thrasher, Clifford Shaw, and Henry McKay in the 1930's on the organization and behavior of delinquent gangs shed new light on the importance of social factors in producing collective acts of deviance. After World War II, interest in explaining deviant youth cultures was renewed. Albert Cohen's statement of key theoretical issues in 1955 has stimulated much research on the composition, distribution, and development of delinquent activity among lower-class youths. More recently, as might be expected, sociologists have turned their attention to middle-class drug-using groups, hippie cults, protest movements, and urban riots. As a result of this turn in interest, the fields of deviance and collective behavior have moved closer to one another in the past decade.

As these new theoretical perspectives have emerged, investigators have redefined their topics of interest. Instead of studying prostitutes or criminals, they have turned to more analytic categories: the offender, the victim, the reactions of agents of social control, social definitions of deviant behavior, the norms that are being violated, the norms that support the deviant act, and the resources and opportunities for deviant behavior.

## The Offender

Most studies of deviance concentrate on the personalities, the backgrounds, and the current situations of offenders as these differ from those of non-offenders. Perhaps the most exhaustive and painstaking study of this kind was completed by Sheldon and Eleanor Glueck in the 1950's. This was a comparative analysis of 500 delinquents, with a matched sample of 500 non-delinquents from the same neighborhoods. Cultural, national, racial, and class differences between the two groups were held constant. The greatest differences that emerged from the enormous numbers of computations were that the delinquents had more often been subjected to lax, vacillating, or over-strict discipline than to firm but patient discipline, and that the delinquents often did not have close affectional ties to the father or the mother.

Though sociologists have expended much effort on these studies, the solid results have been limited. One handicap has been the inability to define and sample a realistic universe of offenders, such as drug users. The sample is typically drawn from persons defined as deviant by some public agency, such as the police or the courts. As our vignette on crime victimization (Chapter 1) demonstrated, however, this method of sampling leaves many offenders undetected or unreported.

To overcome this handicap, some investigators have attempted to survey different groups in order to elicit anonymous or confidential self-reports of deviant activity. For example, one study of a sample of nearly 1,700 adults, mainly from the state of New York, revealed that 99 percent of the respondents admitted to acts for which they might have been jailed. In fact, 64 percent of the males and 29 percent of the females in the sample admitted to felonious acts for which they had not been apprehended.

Though these studies also suffer from many methodological problems, they have helped to reveal some of the biases in official statistics. An intensive study of youth in a medium-size city found that, while participation in minor acts of delinquency is very widespread, involvement in serious and frequent acts of deviance is heavily concentrated in families and neighborhoods with multiple social problems. Despite their apparent advantages over studies based on official statistics, however, self-report studies have not disclosed systematic differences between offenders and non-offenders. In consequence, research workers have redirected their efforts to studying the social careers of deviants and the social context of deviance rather than simply the initial acts of delinquency.

In contrast to the mass of work on the individual offender, relatively little effort has been made to explain the deviant actions of organizations—price-fixing conspiracies, consumer fraud, or black-market activities, for example. This circumstance is an odd one, since the study of the illegitimate activities of organizations presumably brings distinctively sociological as well as psychological concepts to bear on their explanation. This curious neglect of distinctively sociological phenomena by sociologists must remain, for the moment, unexplained. Their importance, however, continues to be evident.

### The Victim

Most crimes have victims—as in homicide, burglary, rape, and fraud. In many cases the victim is an innocent and helpless bystander, but very little is known about those cases in which he plays a role in the escalation of an encounter into a crime. When does this occur? Does the victim play a role in the commission of an offense? We know little about these questions; but answers to them will contribute much to understanding the dynamics of criminal events.

Not all crimes have victims, however. Some involve "deals" between a client and the purveyor of some illicit good or service—as in abortion, homosexuality, prostitution, pornography, drug sales, gambling, and graft payments. In earlier decades sociologists tended to regard these willing accomplices as victims—that is, they emphasized the plight of the client who desires illicit gratifications. More recently, however, sociologists have concentrated on the relations between parties to these arrangements and public authorities. One of the most interesting features of these "crimes without victims" is that law-enforcement officials frequently engage in undercover practices, such as hiring informants and outright bribery, to ferret out activities about which the involved parties seldom complain. The result is a kind of sociological paradox: the development of "secondary deviance" in order to control "primary deviance." Many recent studies have attempted to discover the complex relations that develop between clients, sellers, and enforcers.

### The System of Social Control

Many agencies of social control—the public and private police, prosecutors and defenders, civil and criminal courts, and correctional and treatment agencies—have been insufficiently studied. The police and the courts have been especially neglected, though several exploratory studies have inquired into the organizational problems faced by these agencies, as well as the delicate processes involved in their exercise of discretionary decisions. Sociologists have also studied the adult and juvenile correctional services and the mental hospitals fairly intensively in the past fifteen years. For example, Erving Goffman's study of asylums has revealed that mental patients have characteristic careers and emerging self-orientations that are shaped in large part by their encounters with doctors, nurses, attendants, and other patients. More recently these studies have begun to compare the effects of different kinds of treatment on the self-definition, individual behavior, and collective responses of the client groups.

One of the most promising lines of recent investigation has been the exploration of the ways in which agencies of social control may exaggerate the very types of deviance they are attempting to control. Some sociological investigators have argued, for example, that to label a youth as "delinquent" or a patient as "sick" may work in some ways to create the very condition that has been so labeled. Many of these studies, reacting against the uncritical acceptance of legal and medical judgments as gospel, have been negatively polemical against authorities and normative systems. It now appears that studies that fall between the "pro-system" and "pro-deviant" approaches should be encouraged—studies that objectively analyze the interaction between the behavior of those who are judged to be offenders and those who are doing the judging.

## The Norms That Are Violated

Lawyers, economists, sociologists, and political scientists are beginning to study the origin, development, and institutionalization of official norms and sanctions. They are asking questions about the dynamics of the creation of new laws that define activities as deviant, the role of "moral entrepreneurs" in the creation of these laws, and the dynamics of public reaction to deviant conduct. Such questions will occupy an important place in the research of sociologists of deviance in the decades to come.

## The Norms of Deviant Groups

A regular feature of deviant behavior is that deviants legitimize their behavior by reference to some private or collective series of counter-norms, which they set against the norms they conceive to exist in the larger society. When these counter-norms become institutionalized in a deviant group, a deviant subculture is formed, a subculture that encourages the development and maintenance of deviant careers. For example, when a subculture of professional theft develops, it provides a milieu within which thieves may be recruited, trained, and professionalized. Sociologists are well aware of the power of deviant subcultures and their power to fashion the behavior of deviants, but they have not yet discovered the particular circumstances that converge to create and perpetuate these subcultures.

## Opportunities for Deviance

Most people who think about deviance assume that the principal characteristic of an offender is that he *wants* to break the law or that he *wants* to offend public morality. They think less often about his capacity or his resources to do so. But, in fact, it is true of illegitimate activities as it is of legitimate ones that in order to do one's deed one must have the opportunity as well as the will to do it. A person must be chosen, trained, promoted, and given the opportunity for illegitimate as well as legitimate acts. Some good descriptive work has been done—such as that of Edwin Sutherland—on the professional thief. But too little is known about the ways in which limited opportunities condition the behavior of the car thief, the bank robber, the loan shark, and others.

### Theory of Deviant Behavior

It is one thing to identify the components of deviant behavior—the offender, the victim, the norms that are violated, the norms of the deviant group, and the opportunities for deviance. It is another to view these as interacting in some systematic way to produce a deviant act or a deviant subculture. Social psychologists are beginning to attack this difficult enterprise by attempting to map the field of determinants that influence the deviant act. Sociologists are beginning to attempt to order the determinants into sequential process models. It is too early to ascertain whether these efforts will bear fruit. But the need for them, as well as their promise, is sufficiently great to justify continued and increased support of them.

## SOCIAL CHANGE

American society has always been dynamic. Its traditional values stress active mastery and initiative; it has had the opportunity for explosive growth by virtue of an abundance of resources and frontiers; and it has had to absorb millions of migrants from different cultures during its two centuries of history. We are, moreover, still in the throes of rapid change. Consider only the enormous changes in the role of government in the past forty years, the potency of forces like the civil rights movement, and the extraordinary and continuing transformation of life occasioned by the concentration of the populace in sprawling cities. It comes as no surprise that many sociologists direct their analysis toward processes of social change and social problems arising from change.

The activities of sociologists who focus on change can be grouped conveniently, if somewhat arbitrarily, under three headings: (1) the study of collective behavior, including crowd behavior and social movements; (2) the study of large-scale institutional changes, especially in modernizing societies; and (3) historical sociology. Each area has shown some vitality since World War II, and each promises to thrive in the coming decades.

## Collective Behavior

The term "collective behavior" encompasses the study of phenomena such as collective panics and crazes, fads and fashions, crowd behavior, reform and revolutionary movements, and the like. Sociologists and psychologists pose a wide array of questions about these dramatic episodes. What motivates participation in collective outbursts and collective movements? What social conditions are most likely to produce collective protest? Why do riots and other disturbances erupt in some cities and not in others? Why do some revolutionary movements succeed and others flounder? Do people develop a special "mentality" in crowd situations, and, if so, what are its characteristics and how does it arise? Are people in crowds especially subject to emotional appeals and manipulation by leaders? How do the actions of police, public officials, and other agents of social control affect the development of episodes of collective behavior?

The past century is rich in theoretical speculations on these questions. Yet the field of collective behavior has scarcely been cumulative from the standpoints of substantive findings, research methods, and theoretical adequacy. Only in the past decade has it shown signs of attaining scientific standing. It has been carried on by a relatively small number of sociologists who, at some point in their training, have been exposed to and attracted by the problems this elusive area presents. Their work has been done in relative isolation; they have produced an extensive but fugitive literature; and, in the absence of financial support, they have seldom been able to recruit large numbers of qualified graduate students. The historical explanation for the sluggish growth of the subject is no doubt complex. But a part of any explanation is the fact that people, including both social scientists and those in a position to support them, generally have very strong personal reactions to episodes of collective behavior, and consequently they tend to blame and take sides. Such reactions are not conducive to the dispassionate frame of mind that is necessary if the investigator is to collect and analyze his data within a scientific framework.

Despite its deficiencies, developments within the field—as well as the rise in public concern over protest and violence—have helped to spark a renaissance of interest in collective behavior among sociologists and others during the past decade. Since 1955 several ambitious and general volumes on the subject have appeared—one emphasizing group process, another the collective redefinitions of social situations, another the social conditions underlying collective outbursts and movements, and still another the application of formal mathematical models to collective episodes. One effect of this renewed theoretical interest has been to encourage sociologists to think of collective behavior not as something isolated or bizarre, but rather as something to which the usual array of sociological concepts and research tools can be applied.

Simultaneously, scholars from many disciplines have produced an impressive number of theoretically relevant case studies. Historians have described medieval millenarian movements and crowds in revolutionary situations. Political scientists have studied the development of new parties and extremist protest movements. Anthropologists have analyzed the temperance movement, passive resistance, and the development of religious cults. A few sociologists have studied urban violence comparatively in an effort to locate underlying social conditions and precipitating factors. This new wave of research has been conducted at a level not seen before in the study of collective behavior.

Signs of more solid institutional support for collective-behavior research are also appearing. At least one university has established a privately funded research center for the study of violence; the National Crime Commission and the National Institute of Mental Health have supported some research on mass violence; and the President's advisory commissions on civil disorder and violence have relied on professional sociologists for research staff and periodic consultation. Needless to say, the discrepancy between the need for sociological expertise in these areas and the existing supply of expertise is enormous.

In sum, collective behavior is a field showing new signs of life, and is badly in need of nourishment to capitalize on this initial momentum. Increased communication among scholars in diverse disciplines, who

have done most of their work in relative isolation, is an essential require-
ment, as are new kinds of data-gathering, such as (a) a continuous check
on phenomena like riots, rumors, and public sentiments; (b) occasional
and pointed observations in connection with community "moods" and
other evasive data; and (c) the establishment of "fire-house" brigades
to move to the scene of episodes of collective behavior as they unfold.
And finally, it is necessary to encourage the budding interest in applying formal models to processes of collective behavior.

## Modernization

One of the oldest and most enduring preoccupations in sociology is the pattern of institutional changes that unfold when a society
moves from a simple to a complex form. Most of the founding fathers of
modern sociology—including Auguste Comte, Karl Marx, Herbert
Spencer, Émile Durkheim, William Graham Sumner, and Charles
Horton Cooley—analyzed these processes of change in one way or another. Most of their theories, however, rested either on oversimple
evolutionary assumptions or oversimple dichotomies between traditional
and modern society. Thus these theories tended to fall short of dynamic
or causal explanation of change, though they often produced brilliant
insights. Furthermore, they too often rested on little or no solid empirical research, and were very speculative, especially with respect to simple
societies. Because of these and other shortcomings, the classical theories
of institutional change fell into disfavor around the turn of the century.

After World War II, sociology witnessed an energetic revival of interest in social change, especially modernization. Part of the impetus for
this change came from a renewed theoretical interest in the works of
Durkheim and Weber by many American sociologists. More important
were the end of colonization, the emergence of the "new nations," and
the great turmoil that has accompanied the efforts of these nations to
join the modern world. Social scientists in several disciplines found
themselves limited to the analysis of advanced market economies of the
West and in need of new assumptions and knowledge about social and
cultural change. Political scientists, with a framework designed mainly
to study political processes in developed societies, found themselves
limited in their ability to deal with non-Western political systems, par-

ticularly those in rapid flux. And finally, sociologists and anthropologists, who a half-century earlier had been preoccupied with social changes accompanying industrialization and urbanization, discovered that the atrophy of these interests had left them poorly equipped to understand the developing nations.

Facing this glaring need for new knowledge and understanding, social scientists have carried out a most impressive quantity of research on institutional changes in the developing nations during the past twenty years. The level of financial support for research, emanating from universities, private foundations, and the federal government has been equally impressive. Many universities have established research centers for the study of special regions or cultural areas. Others have established centers for comparative international studies. Both these kinds of research centers have concentrated their research on problems of institutional change.

Research has covered the most diverse topics. In this report we have already pointed to William J. Goode's study of comparative changes in family structure under the impact of industrialization and urbanization, demographic research on the alarming imbalance between the changes in mortality and fertility rates in the developing countries, and the comparative institutional analyses of Marion J. Levy, Jr. and Barrington Moore, Jr. Other sociologists and anthropologists have attempted to assess the relevance of the "Weber thesis"—that ascetic Protestantism was especially conducive to the growth of capitalism in the West—for the newly developing societies, by careful examination of their religious systems and the religious backgrounds of entrepreneurs. Numerous sociologists and political scientists have isolated groups in the population of developing countries that play critical roles in fomenting social and political instability—groups like unemployed intellectuals, workers in transition from traditional labor roles to wage labor, and the floating mass of urban unemployed. To mention a final illustration, sociologists and political scientists alike have traced the emergence of new organizational forms—political bureaucracies, business firms, and labor unions—and they have analyzed the dynamic balance between modern structural requirements and traditional practices. Monographs, case studies, and essays on the diverse aspects of modernization number in the thousands.

Yet despite the great vitality of research on institutional changes in modernizing societies, progress in the area has been impeded by a number of factors. On the *theoretical* side, there has been a failure to achieve sufficiently fine distinctions among a variety of general processes—modernization, economic development, social development—and the components that go into each process. Investigators have tended to study either quantitative rates (such as per capita output or level of literacy), structural changes (such as the growth of bureaucracy), or cultural changes (such as secularization or the growth of new political ideologies). But the fundamental relations among these several types of changes have scarcely been conceptualized, much less discovered. Even though models and theories have proliferated, the social sciences have not yet witnessed sufficient theoretical innovation in the study of change to overcome these fundamental shortcomings.

On the *empirical* side, the systematic study of change continues to be plagued by a number of methodological difficulties. We reviewed a number of methodological problems that are posed by the comparative analysis of large-scale systems in our brief discussion of the comparative study of societies. More specifically, the comparative study of change—essential for the development of adequate theory—is impeded by the lack of standardized time series. Most of the developing countries have only recently begun to record social data systematically, so that many series extend only a few decades into the past. Furthermore, these data are diverse and unstandardized, which is frustrating to the investigator in search of comparable indices. It is urgent to encourage the work of international agencies that attempt to produce standardized series. It is equally urgent to work toward establishing a number of international research and archive centers that could devote their energies to gathering and recording standardized social data over long periods of time.

We add a final note on the interdisciplinary aspects of the study of modernization. The revitalization of interest since World War II has been notable for the great overlap of interest and collaboration among anthropologists, sociologists, and political scientists, and, to a lesser degree, economists and historians. Part of this need for interdisciplinary interest stems from the subject-matter itself. When a society is undergoing changes as complex as those involved in modernization, the scholar cannot escape the fact that everything is changing at once, and he cannot escape the need to know something about the other aspects of change in order to understand his own specific aspect. Because these scholars are driven to move beyond the boundaries of their own disciplines, we suspect that modernization is an especially promising area from the standpoint of theoretical integration among the social and behavioral sciences.

## Historical Sociology

A final trend in recent research on social change is the effort of a number of scholars to bring sociological concepts, theories, and research methods to bear on historical questions. It would be difficult and probably pointless to assign this type of research to either sociology or history, since scholars in both fields have contributed to the trend.

Historical sociology has its origins in nineteenth-century German and French scholarship. A notable sociological classic is Alexis de Tocqueville's analysis of the *ancien régime* and the French Revolution. The scientific aspects of this tradition of research are the use of statistical methods for dealing with quantitative problems, systematic exploration and codification of archival sources, preoccupation with methodological problems, careful attention to the relevance of materials for theoretical issues, and suspension of value judgments insofar as possible while gathering and analyzing historical information.

Contemporary historical sociologists have inherited this tradition, and have made more effective use of evolving sociological theories and research methods. A sample of disciplined historical studies would include Charles Tilly's study of the Vendée counter-revolution, Kai Erikson's study of deviance in the Puritan colonial period, Robert Bellah's study of religion and social change in Tokugawa Japan, E. Digby Baltzell's historical studies of aristocracies, Reinhard Bendix's historical study of authority relations in Great Britain, the United States, East Germany, and Russia, and Stephen Thernstrom's study of patterns of social mobility in Newburyport in the nineteenth century—on the basis of which he criticized from a historical standpoint materials gathered by W. Lloyd Warner for his Yankee City series. Most of these books are the products of library research by a solitary scholar, but some investigators are making use of complex quantitative processing of historical data, computer simulations, and retrieval systems. The uses of these techniques are especially conspicuous in demographic and economic history.

Historical sociology has been given additional impetus by the establishment of joint graduate training programs in history, by the appearance of "comparative history" programs in history departments, and by the appearance of a few specialized journals devoted to reporting the results of research in historical sociology.

These new developments in historical sociology have occurred without substantial financial support from funding agencies. Most of the research has been supported by the universities themselves, in the form of sabbatical leaves, fellowships, and extensive library facilities. Recently some private foundations and federal agencies—notably the National Science Foundation—have begun to extend modest support to research projects in historical sociology. This marks a departure from the tradition of regarding historical research as humanistic rather than scientific. We welcome this support, and encourage its extension, because it facilitates inquiry into an important dimension of sociological analysis and consolidates a bridge between the disciplines of sociology and history.

## POLITICAL SOCIOLOGY

### The Field and Its Focus

Political sociology is a very old subject, extending as far back as the moral and political philosophers who first began to fathom the complex relations between the polity and the society within which it is embedded. Most of the founding fathers of sociology, moreover, found it impossible to write about societies without soon raising questions about the political order. Political sociology as a major field in the discipline, however, has emerged only recently. Not until after World War II was a definite and self-conscious tradition of research established and not until then did some sociologists begin to preface their professional titles with the word "political" and to offer courses in their new specialty.

Sociologists of politics focus their research on a variety of questions. What conditions in society promote political order and political disorder, respectively? Why are some political systems regarded as legitimate, others as illegitimate, by citizens? Why are some political systems stable, others unstable? Why are some governments democratic, others totalitarian, still others a mixture of the two? What determines variations in party systems, levels of political participation, and rates of voting? In attempting to throw light on these questions political sociologists have relied on that great variety of research methods available to the field as a whole—comparative analysis of social systems, historical description, analysis of aggregated survey data, and on occasion, participant observation.

## Lines of Research Interest

One of the most vital areas of interest in political sociology concerns what has come to be called "political development"—those changes in political values and political institutions that unfold as nations attempt to modernize themselves. Typical of these changes is political differentiation, or the emergence of relatively separate and autonomous political structures. Prior to the beginning of rapid development many societies have relatively undifferentiated structures. Men at the heads of political systems are simultaneously the dominant religious leaders and at the summit of the economic class structures. Rapid economic and social changes accompanying modernization foster a breakdown in fixed class or caste relations and encourage a separation between religion and politics. At the same time the political exigencies of the society become increasingly demanding and this paves the way for the emergence of new political structures—such as parties and civil service systems—and new patterns of political participation. Gino Germani's studies of Argentine development, for example, have revealed two broad consequences of urbanization: the weakening of the authority of the traditional landed elite who also resided in cities and owned industry and the creation of a new lower-class stratum of hundreds of thousands of migrants to the cities. As peasants the latter group had not been politically active, but, once urbanized, they became potential supporters of extremist, mass-based political movements.

As the spiral toward modernization continues, the need for a bigger and busier government grows correspondingly. Governments begin to take responsibilities for creating an educated populace, without which economic growth is inhibited. They typically take the leadership in smashing traditional vested interests—such as caste and tribal elites—that may be antipathetic to modernization. They must assume leadership in striving to improve the international power and prestige of their countries. In these ways economic, social, and political mobilization go hand in hand and in the developing countries the political system plays a central role in all three processes.

Often the effort to untangle the causes underlying economic and political development turns up unanticipated results. It has been discovered, for example, that reforms required for development cause a *decline* of economic productivity and an *increase* in political instability in the short run. In Latin America, for example, programs of breaking up large landholdings have the immediate effect of lowering rural productivity because the small owners cannot mobilize the capital resources available to the large owners. A survey of attitudes toward guerrilla activity in Vietnam uncovered the fact that areas enjoying recent land reform showed *more* support for the Viet Cong than did those areas that have retained the backward system of semi-feudal tenancy. Though many causes undoubtedly work to produce this effect, it is likely that land reform upsets the social relations that support traditional values and leaves the peasantry open to new and often radical values.

The sociologist's interest in social change and political stability leads him quickly to questions of political legitimacy—which refers to the degree to which significant groups in the society accept the existing political system of decision-making as binding, whether or not they agree with its policies. Most nations face crises of legitimacy from time to time, as we know from our familiarity with the Great Revolutions of Europe—the British in 1642, the French in 1789, the upheavals in many nations in 1848, and the Russian in 1917—as well as our own Revolutionary and Civil Wars. Crises of legitimacy are especially evident in the developing countries, where the people have no traditional reason for accepting regimes as having an enduring, morally justified claim to their allegiance. Crises of legitimacy are also likely to be severe during the period immediately after government has risen by revolutionary overthrow. Under these conditions of equivocal legitimacy, the military is likely to play a critical role in determining whether a regime remains in power, falls dramatically, or is replaced quietly by a new regime. Morris Janowitz' research on developing nations has documented the significance of the military in determining the political fate of governments in these nations.

In their comparative studies political sociologists have advanced—and documented to some degree—the hypothesis that one major condition for maintaining legitimacy is to separate the *source* of legitimacy from the *agencies* responsible for carrying out day-by-day policies. An example is the separation of our own Constitution, from which legitimacy derives, from partisan political competition; another is the separation of the British monarchy from the politics of the day. Though the mechanisms underlying this hypothesis are not perfectly understood, it is probable that the resultant political stability traces to the fact that people are able to express negative sentiments toward the immediate holders of power (presidents, congressmen, prime ministers, for example) without at the same time attacking their sources of legitimacy (the Constitution, the Crown).

Despite this insight, the ultimate sources of legitimacy are not well understood. The topic remains one of the highest priority in sociology, particularly since it is so clearly a major problem for almost every nation in the modern world.

Politics—like parenthood—is one of those arenas of social life in which actions designed to have a specific effect—such as jailing a member of an opposition group, or spanking a disobedient child—may backfire and lead to consequences that were unanticipated by the perpetrator of the act. Political sociologists have made this social truth a major subject for investigation. Following the lead of theorists like Max Weber and Robert Michels, they have attempted to analyze the ways in which policy-makers' most cherished intentions may be changed or even negated in the process of implementation. Research of sociologists has documented dozens of ways in which "company policy" is systematically modified in bureaucratic structures. Given the fact that bureaucracy has become the organizational means by which industrial societies operate, knowledge of the forces that determine variations in bureaucratic functioning in different societies is crucial.

Just as sociologists have investigated the ways in which policies are (or are not) implemented, so they have been concerned with the operation of the forces—party politics, voting behavior, social movements, public opinion, interest groups—that influence the formation of these policies. Students of party politics, for example, have asked how social class, religious preference, and ethnic and regional differences have led to the formation of and support for different types of party systems. Students of voting behavior have attempted to trace the impact of various group memberships—religious affiliation, labor union membership, and the like—on voters' choices of candidates and parties. Early research emphasized the impact of more enduring determinants, such as social class. More recently, scholars have attempted to assess the effects of variables more specific to a given electoral campaign—variables such as the issues, the events that occur during the campaign, or the candidates themselves. A number of simulated models of the voting decision have also facilitated the analysis of variations in electoral results.

Studies of political participation, above and beyond voting, are central to political sociology, because they reveal the ways in which different groups and strata influence authorities' decisions. These studies have shown consistently that the level of political participation is closely associated with a person's place in the stratification system: the well-to-do, the educated, and the prestigious participate more in voting, writing letters, speaking to decision-makers, lobbying, and so on. The reasons for this are not altogether clear. Perhaps it is because those with lower income and status know less about the consequences of participation, possess fewer skills and resources, and suspect that they are less likely to evoke responses from authorities than are those higher in the stratification system. Findings such as these indicate that the establishment of policies like "maximum feasible participation of the poor" requires more than simple legislation; it also requires an understanding of the social conditions that might facilitate, inhibit, or deny effective participation.

Political sociology is one of those sub-divisions of the discipline that has clearly already experienced its "take-off" toward scientific maturity, and considerable scientific research is being carried forward both by sociologists and political scientists. Their findings in the areas reviewed, while promising, are clearly far from definitive. Key conceptual areas like the definition of power, characterization of the relations between consensus and conflict, and the nature of political socialization are still underdeveloped. On the empirical side, even voting behavior, which has been studied with the most sophisticated quantitative techniques, is still largely unexplained; research in this field can account for less than half of the variance in aggregated voting rates. Political sociology, in short, is one of the fields that has gained a degree of momentum, which continued and expanded support could greatly accelerate.

## SOCIOLOGY OF EDUCATION

The sociology of education is one of the fastest-growing fields in the discipline. It is now one of the three specialties with its own journal sponsored by the American Sociological Association (the others are social psychology and the sociology of mental health and illness), and is becoming a popular field for doctoral specialization, both in sociology departments and in schools of education.

### Education as a Sociological Variable

The level and kind of an individual's education has long been recognized as one of the most important pervasive influences on the other aspects of his life. Education, along with occupation and income, are key components of socio-economic status. Sociologists of stratification have analyzed the strong and complex relations among these three variables. Their studies have shown that it is easy to predict the social prestige of an occupation from the average income and education of those pursuing the occupation. This also means that a society's educational system is closely related to its system of stratification—an important truth for a nation seeking equal opportunity for its citizens. In particular, recent research has pinpointed the crucial role that educational attainment plays in determining whether sons get better, worse, or similar jobs in comparison with their fathers. In statistical language, it has been demonstrated that when sons' educational attainment is controlled, the correlation between the prestige levels of fathers' and sons' jobs is low. In non-statistical terms, this means that American fathers influence their sons' occupational levels mainly by affecting their sons' educational attainments.

Educational attainment is also a strong indicator of attitudes and opinions. It has been shown to be related to political opinions, patterns of taste and interest in civic, national, and world affairs. Level of education is strongly and positively correlated with degree of liberalism in inter-racial and free-speech questions (though less so on economic issues). Less obviously, some studies have shown that education is correlated with mental-health measures, with the better educated tending to score higher on various measures of adjustment.

Educational attainment is related to behavior as well as attitudes. For example, knowing about the education of people, we can predict the likely characteristics of their family life. Highly educated people marry later and have more stable marriages. And the famous Kinsey research showed that people at different educational levels show considerable differences in their sexual behavior, though this applies to men more than to women. In the past education and family size have been negatively correlated, but as modern contraceptive techniques have spread from the educated to the uneducated, this difference appears to be diminishing. Some sociologists predict that it will eventually reverse.

Since education affects so many other aspects of life, sociologists have evinced considerable interest in the factors influencing how much education a person receives. Much of the research on this question has been done by psychologists and educators, but sociological studies have shown that parents' socioeconomic status and parental encouragement affect young people's educational aspirations above and beyond other variables such as IQ scores or grades. Much more needs to be known in this area. While grades, IQ, and parental factors are known to be related to educational attainment, their predictive power is so weak that other variables must be found to improve our understanding of this important social process.

Sociologists have also attempted to analyze the nation's aggregate changes in educational attainment over long periods of time. Census figures, of course, reveal a steady increase in educational attainment during the last century, particularly at the elementary and high school levels. However, recent re-analyses of these data have raised questions about whether a high school graduate's chances of entering college are really improving, or whether the expansion in college enrollments is more a reflection of population growth and burgeoning numbers of high school graduates.

So much for illustrations of the pervasiveness of education as a general variable in sociology. The sociology of education proper deals with roles, organizations, and structures specializing in society's educational functions. Research in the field can be grouped under the headings: (1) schools and school systems, and (2) educational occupations.

## Schools and School Systems

Since schools are meant to change people, the question of how different school experiences affect students is a key problem for sociologists. As with so many key problems, less is known than we would hope to know, and we are far from the day when sociologists can advise school planners authoritatively. Nevertheless, this is a lively field for research.

The differences between education in racially segregated and racially integrated schools has attracted the attention of sociologists as well as many other interested parties. Beyond the moral principles involved, it is important to measure the favorable and unfavorable consequences for both races of integrated and segregated schools. Several large-scale studies have been completed recently and others are in progress. It is difficult to generalize from these studies, because every community faces unique problems with respect to racial issues in education. But most findings indicate that integration has some favorable effects, especially for black students, and there is little convincing evidence that it has consistently unfavorable effects for students of either race. With respect to "religious integration," sociologists have also studied public and parochial (mainly Roman Catholic) schools. Recent national surveys have compared the education of Catholics who attended parochial schools with that of Catholics who attended public schools. Some differences appeared, but as is so often the case, these differences were less pronounced than those alleged by both proponents and opponents of church schools.

Sociologists have also studied the impact of a school's "social climate" on students. For example, a number of studies have demonstrated that, regardless of a high school student's social class background or academic record, he is more likely to plan to go to college if he attends a school where high-status students are in the majority—that is, where the social climate for high educational aspirations is favorable. Other studies have shown a slight but consistent tendency for college students to shift their career plans toward occupations that are popular among the other students on their campuses. A more controversial line of research has suggested that the great emphasis on interscholastic athletics in American high schools is a manifestation of a social climate that is antipathetic to scholarly values.

At the broadest level, American sociologists have been participating in comparative studies of the scholastic performance of young people in different nations. A recent cross-national study of achievement in mathematics revealed a complex pattern of differences—few of which should lead Americans to be complacent about their educational system.

What factors explain the great variations in school systems, curricula, and classroom practices? Why, for instance, are some schools "progressive," others "traditional"? What social factors, other than level of financial resources, affect the amount of money a community spends on schools? Important as these questions are, they have not received much attention from sociologists. Perhaps this is because historians and educationists have pre-empted the field; but perhaps it is also because, in our ignorance of how schools actually work, we do not know how to ask the right kinds of questions.

### Educational Occupations

One of the most obvious questions to ask about education is "What makes a good teacher?" Oddly enough, there are few sociological studies of this question, and those that exist yield equivocal results. This does not mean, however, that such research would start from scratch. Hundreds, if not thousands of studies by investigators in the field of education have asked the question. But it remains unsolved, possibly because the same teacher or method will have different results for different students and possibly because it leads to murky philosophical problems in defining the goals of education.

What determines people's decisions to enter educational occupations? Sociologists who investigate career choice and occupational patterns have a long history of studying teachers and have recently taken an interest in studying school administrators.

Surveys of college students have pinpointed the characteristics of those attracted to elementary and high school teaching. It comes as no surprise that the best predictor is being a girl. But, in addition, recruits to classroom teaching are characterized by a pattern of altruistic values, by modest academic records, and by particular social origins (they tend to be less urban and from lower socioeconomic levels). Surveys of new teachers have also shown a pattern of attrition when the beginner's idealism is eroded by the realities of the classroom, paycheck, and school system. Other studies of school superintendents have made clear the complex interplay of political, social, and personal forces involved in this high-pressure job. Professors themselves have finally become an object of inquiry. Sociologists have studied their social origins, their reactions to the McCarthy era of the 1950's, and even the delicate blend of rumor, avarice, status seeking and interpersonal contacts involved in the hiring and firing of faculty members.

Both the impetus of the past decade and the increasing need for solid research justify the prediction that research on educational roles, organizations, and systems will continue to increase rapidly. The educational system itself has grown explosively and promises to continue to experience both rapid growth and its attendant pains. And as it grows and changes shape, it will penetrate even more deeply into the vast range of racial, religious, and political problems facing the nation. The knowledge of educational processes and their place in society clearly stands high on the priority list of both the discipline and the nation.

## MEDICAL SOCIOLOGY

The sociology of health and medical care, like the sociology of education, has recently experienced a remarkable growth. While significant theoretical statements and items of research on health and medicine can be traced back as much as a half-century, the field has become formally designated and systematically elaborate only in the past two decades. So rapid has been the expansion that the section on "medical sociology" in the American Sociological Association has one of the largest memberships—730 members, second only to social psychology with 920, as of August, 1968. No small part of this recent history, moreover, must be traced to the generosity of a Congress that has been aware of the enormity of the social problems associated with illness and to the research policies of various funding agencies, especially the National Institutes of Health and the National Institute of Mental Health.

Medical sociology is neither a strictly "applied" field of sociology nor an analytically-defined field such as socialization or stratification. It occupies a status somewhere between the two. On the one hand it can be regarded as a loosely interrelated collection of investigations in which many of the theories and findings of sociology are applied to the specific problems of health and medical practice. Viewed from this perspective, medical sociology does not have a unified definition or a distinctive theoretical focus. On the other hand, medical sociology can be regarded as focusing on a set of exigencies—the creation and preservation of health—that pose a problem for all societies. Viewed from this perspective, the theoretical focus of medical sociology would be on health and disease as they are defined and dealt with in various societies. In fact, theory in medical sociology is at present only in a very rudimentary stage of development. The attention of sociologists of health and medical care have tended more to organize their research around a number of major areas of interest. Let us review these several areas.

## The Definition and Patterning of Illness Behavior in Society

No individual and no society can be indifferent to the phenomena of pain and disease, since both individual functioning and social processes are so manifestly disrupted by its onset. Every society, moreover, has its "folk medicine" which may or may not be scientifically based. That is to say, each society has identifiable cultural "theories" relating to the nature and origins of diseases. Some societies, for example, regard contamination from menstrual blood as a source of many diseases. Every society also has prescriptions about what should be done by whom when illness attacks. And finally, every society develops norms that designate proper emotional responses both for the person who is ill and for those near him. One of the main tasks of the sociology of medicine is to sort out the ways in which a society's value system, its demographic structure, and its scientific technology combine to determine the ways in which pain and illness are designated and treated. Needless to say, progress on this task will require an ambitious program of comparative empirical research, both across and within societies.

## The Epidemiology of Disease and Impairment

Long before the advent of sociology, people recognized that disease is not distributed at random throughout the social structure. Epidemiologists have carefully documented the differential distribution of disease according to variables like population density, age, sex, socioeconomic status, race, and ethnic background. The distinctive sociological interest in epidemiology arises from the study of the interplay among social, psychological, biological, and physical factors in the determination of any given disease.

While the sociologist can perform a distinctive service by identifying the ways in which social experience affects health and illness, it is evident that his work on epidemiological topics—as on so many topics in medical sociology—requires collaboration with specialists in medicine, psychiatry, psychology, economics, and other disciplines. The sociologist may be aware that tuberculosis is more common in one ethnic group than in others. But before he can fathom the precise features of the life of the ethnic group that are responsible, he must learn what the clinician and epidemiologist already know about the etiology of the disease. At the same time the sociologist's descriptions help the clinician and epidemiologist by offering clues in their search for more precise understanding of its causes.

The study of epidemiology also underscores the great need for longitudinal research. Only so much knowledge can be gained by cross-sectional studies of distributions by social class, ethnic group, religious affiliation, social mobility, and other social categories, without discerning how these distributions unfold over time. Only so much knowledge can be gained from case studies in hospitals, which often cannot be generalized beyond the case itself. Systematic longitudinal studies are required to isolate and analyze antecedent life experiences that presumably affect health. Without such studies it is difficult to determine, for example, whether low socioeconomic status is conducive to schizophrenia, or whether a pre-schizophrenic condition forced the individual downward on the socioeconomic scale. While valuable in general, such longitudinal studies are especially important for the study of chronic diseases, which virtually involve the individual in a "sick way of life" with his social and cultural surroundings for extended periods of time.

## Personal and Societal Response to Illness

Both the incidence of disease and the adequacy of medical treatment depend in large part on individual and social definitions of illness. In daily life we observe great differences in people's reactions to what are in fact the same organic symptoms—the hyper-masculine type, for example, who refuses to admit that he has been sick a day in his life, or the hysterical type who rushes to the doctor at the slightest twinge of pain. While such stereotypes are often overdrawn, they do suggest the importance of personal style and social background in the response to illness. People will vary in their readiness to admit illness and receive treatment according to their religious convictions, their trust or distrust of doctors, and their own particular "theories" of medicine.

The social class of the patient is also important. A person of low socioeconomic status normally receives his treatment in a clinic, where he is likely to be cast in a role inferior to the doctor and other medical personnel. Because of these circumstances, and because he is likely to be less articulate than the doctor, he is likely to be unable to clarify his symptoms or understand what the doctor tells him. Some investigators have pointed out that poor communication resulting from status differences may adversely affect the diagnosis of the patient's mental condition. Occupational differences are often important as well. The farmer and the laborer, for example, are less likely to be aware of farsightedness than the scholar.

Because the definition of disease and treatment are subject to such great individual and social differences, the measurement of the incidence and the nature of disease becomes very complicated. So long as a condition—such as recurrent indigestion or seasonal "hay fever"—is regarded by some as illness and by others as a troublesome moment in an otherwise healthy existence, efforts to measure its incidence face great difficulties. Some of the attempts to survey the extent of various diseases and symptoms suffer from these variations in definition of illness, as well as from people's notoriously unreliable memory of their own medical histories. Needless to say, efforts to survey the incidence of mental disorders by self-report are especially vulnerable to these methodological difficulties.

These difficulties underscore the need to provide facilities for standardized and centralized record-keeping of the health of various segments of the population. These facilities would not only be of value to the practitioner, whose diagnoses and treatment are often inadequate because they are based on faulty information provided by his patients. They would also be of great value to scholars and public health workers whose endeavors require thorough and reliable records of the social incidence of illness. For the medical sociologist, the availability of such records would allow him systematically to explore the causal relations between organic symptoms on the one hand, and various psychological and social variables on the other.

## Medical Care in the Society and the Community

The organization of medical services in any society depends on more than the state of development of scientific medicine. It also depends on the general values and norms of the society in question. Depending on cultural and political traditions, one society may opt for a modified "free enterprise" medical system, another for medical insurance, and a third for a completely socialized plan. Sociologists and other social scientists have barely begun to study these arrangements, as well as the conditions under which new systems of medical provision arise in response to other social changes. Another promising area of study is the variation in social status accorded to physicians and other medical personnel in various societies.

Some studies of the diffusion of medical innovations have also been conducted. The study of spread of a wonder drug, summarized earlier, is an example. Yet there is much we do not understand about the dynamics of resistance and gullibility toward innovations. Why does the commercial advertising of a wonder drug sometimes bring demands that are not quelled by authoritative warnings and denials, while fluoridation of the water supplies evokes vigorous opposition? Why are personal habits, such as eating practices, drug use, and exercising, apparently so difficult to change?

Deliberate efforts to improve the health of a population—as in public health campaigns, illness prevention campaigns, and so on—provide an excellent opportunity for research teams to "track" the success of the efforts by carefully constructed field experiments. The method for tracing the impact of an educational family-planning program, described earlier, could be applied to various programs of medical intervention. In conducting such studies, the task for medical sociology would be to discover how various social variables—such as age, sex, education, and ethnic group membership—facilitate or obstruct the effectiveness of these programs. The results would provide us with knowledge of the "epidemiology of prevention and cure" that would correspond to our knowledge concerning the spread of illness itself.

## The Internal Organization of Medical Facilities

Most medical treatment takes place within organizations. Most medical organizations, moreover, involve a large and complex network of personal relationships which affect the course of medical treatment. Conflicts among doctors or between doctors and nurses, for example, have been shown to aggravate certain types of symptoms, especially those associated with mental illness. In addition, the hospital exhibits the usual features of a bureaucracy. It must sustain vertical and horizontal communications; maintain a system of authority, and attend to the morale of its personnel. The hospital also has special organizational problems that stem from the fact that much of its staff is recruited from independent professionals. The physician who becomes a hospital administrator is asked to do a job of organizational coordination, whereas his earlier specialized training has equipped him with an entirely different set of skills. If the hospital hires a professionally trained medical administrator, however, he is likely to experience status inferiority in relation to the doctors over whom he presumably has some authority. The study of hospital administration, in short, offers many opportunities to explore the effects of role ambiguity and role conflict.

The study of the organizational features of medical care has become increasingly urgent in recent years, as individual medical practice on a free basis has given way so rapidly to group practice, larger and more complex hospitals, and insurance and prepayment schemes. Sociologists must not only extend their empirical studies to these new types of organization, but they must also be prepared to revise their traditional conceptual frameworks. Historically the study of the professional role has relied on the model of the "unattached" practitioner, whereas the contemporary scene finds the professional implicated in a complex organizational network. New models of formal organization must also be devised to analyze the delicate and unique mixtures of administrative authority and collegial responsibility that characterize so many roles in the modern hospital.

## The Relationship Between Professional and Patient

Finally, sociologists have taken a special interest in the social roles of medical practitioners and the doctor-patient relationship. This relationship has a number of peculiar features. For example, the physician normally receives a fee for his services whether or not he is successful in curing the patient. The ethics and norms of the relationship also call for great concern for the patient's interests on the part of the physician and great trust of the physician on the part of the patient. These features are felt to be important for the success of all kinds of medical treatment, and especially significant for psychiatric care. Sociologists have written a number of empirical descriptions of variations on these roles, and have ventured a few attempts at explaining why the doctor-patient relationship is structured the way it is.

Yet deeper understanding of this relationship is required, particularly in the light of the increasing bureaucratization and possible depersonalization of medical service and in the light of the expression of distrust of physicians in some quarters. Rising medical costs and the increasing specialization of practice have undoubtedly contributed to these feelings of distrust, as well as to the fear that the patient is at the mercy of the physician. Many new questions must be asked. What is the effect of "middle-men"—receptionists, nurses, technicians—on the relationship between doctor and patient? Under what circumstances will patients seek emotional gratifications beyond those of being cured in the doctor-patient relationship? To what extent do different systems of training and different systems of practice facilitate or impede the development of trust between doctor and patient? What is the impact of "socialized" systems of medical care on the doctor-patient relationship? These and other unanswered questions indicate both the extent of our ignorance and the need for future investigators to press forward in their analysis of this exceptional human relationship.

## OBSTACLES TO THE DEVELOPMENT OF SOCIOLOGICAL KNOWLEDGE: SOME SPECULATIONS ABOUT RELIGION AND RACE

In this chapter we have selected several areas of sociological inquiry that have shown some kind of theoretical or empirical development in the past several decades or a promise of development in the coming years. We could have expanded the list considerably. Unhappily, however, we could not expand it to include all areas of sociological investigation. Some fields in the discipline have remained relatively though not entirely undeveloped from the standpoint of generating an adequate theoretical framework and accumulating a body of reliable empirical findings. We could identify a long list of these fields—the sociology of art and literature, the sociology of race relations, the sociology of the family, the sociology of religion, the sociology of sports and games, the sociology of academic organizations, to name a few. Each of these fields has its own story, and we select only two for illustration: religion and race. Why have these fields lagged in theoretical and empirical development in comparison to areas like stratification, demography, and formal organizations?

In posing this question—and speculating about answers—we mean neither to slight these two fields nor to imply that no good work has been or is being done in them. Quantitatively, the number of books and articles on race that are written by sociologists and people interested in sociology is probably as large as on any comparable field in the discipline. Some of these, moreover, compare well with similar research in other areas. A sample of theoretically relevant and empirically informed studies in the area of race relations would include research in James M. Coleman, *et al.*, *Equality of Educational Opportunity*; Karl E. Taeuber and Alma F. Taeuber's *Negroes in Cities*, a careful quantitative study of residential segregation during the past three decades; Robin Williams' *Strangers Next Door*, a study of racial conflict and tensions in a number of communities; and Gary Marx's *Protest and Prejudice*, a systematic and revealing analysis of survey data concerning Negroes' social attitudes.

In religion as well, sociologists have produced a variety of studies of high quality on such subjects as the changing forms of religious organization, contemporary religious leadership roles, and the nature, sources, and consequences of an individual's religious commitment. A few examples are the works of Gerhard Lenski, Charles Y. Glock, and Rodney Stark, who have made fruitful use of survey data to study the social and attitudinal correlates of religious affiliation and commitment; Robert N. Bellah's comparative studies of religion and social change; and Guy E. Swanson's monographs on the relations between religious and political structure. In addition to these and other notable works, several generations of sociologists have made hundreds of empirical studies in which religion or race has figured as an important variable. Despite all this activity, work in both areas has tended to be generally descriptive, at a low level of theoretical generality; and a general preoccupation with the moral and political aspects of religion and race has overshadowed their scientific analysis.

Nothing inherent in the subject matter of either area would suggest that it should be unimportant for sociological study. Religious sentiments are among the most profound determinants of man's motivation and social behavior. Religious affiliation and commitment, moreover, have been demonstrated to be powerfully associated with a whole range of behavior, including voting, educational performance, and choice of spouses and friends. Moreover, religion is well-represented in the classical works of figures such as Max Weber, Émile Durkheim, Sigmund Freud, and Bronislaw Malinowski. As for race, it has always been one of the most visible and pervasive principles of social organization in American society, and patently something that must be incorporated into any explanatory account of social institutions and social behavior. So we must return to our original question: What factors have tended to impede the scientific development of these fields?

For each field the answer must be viewed as a convergence of forces both within and outside sociology, and to fix the responsibility on either side would be to yield too narrow an account. To begin with religion, sociologists have, by and large, failed to maintain a very high level of interest in religious phenomena, though the reasons for this are not entirely clear. Another obstacle to the development of the field is the reluctance of American sociologists to learn foreign languages. This is understandable, since most of the scholarly literature on the sociology of religion is either originally in English or has been translated. But the unfamiliarity with foreign languages has seriously inhibited the comparative study of non-Western religions, which calls for prolonged training in Arabic, Sanskrit, or Chinese.

Neither has the social and political environment been conducive to the scientific study of religion. First, access to data necessary for scientific investigation is severely restricted. Religious groups are frequently wary about revealing information to a social scientist unless he happens to be a member of unquestioned standing in the faith he is studying. In addition, largely because of the legacy of the separation of church and state, public universities have been slow to establish major departments or research centers for the scientific study of religion. Because of the same legacy, government funding agencies—and most foundations—have been sensitive about supporting research on religious subjects. Other government agencies that are responsible for gathering data have also shied away from anything related to religion. For example, despite the periodic agitation of a small number of sociologists, the Bureau of the Census has not incorporated a question on religious affiliation in the Decennial Census, largely on grounds that compelling an individual to specify his religious affiliation would likely be judged unconstitutional. Whatever the moral and legal merits of this policy, the fact remains that sociologists have been deprived of a source of data that could potentially throw great light on the character of religious life in contemporary society.

Once these various forces converge to relegate a subject like religion to a relatively unscientific status, a further set of forces is set in motion to perpetuate its disadvantaged situation. The study of religion comes to be regarded, quite naturally, as a field which is theoretically and methodologically underdeveloped, and short on findings—a "soft" field, in short. Moreover, because most sociologists want to be social *scientists* above all, they tend to confer little status on fields regarded as soft. As a result, scholars (who are at least as prestige-seeking as other men) are less likely to turn their research interests to topics concerning religion, and students are less likely to enter that specialty. Such is the vicious circle that conspires to keep an unscientific area at an unscientific level of development.

The sociology of religion, then, emerges as a field being carried by a number of dedicated scholars, proceeding largely without financial support from outside, continuing to contribute modestly to our knowledge of man's religious situation. Research in the sociology of religion tends to be parochial, though a few scholars in sociology, anthropology, and history are struggling to break this parochialism and extend the field's boundaries. The field badly needs support for basic research, and the sources of this support must be insulated from variations in public sentiments and political sensitivities. This kind of support is essential if sociologists are to gather and codify relevant religious data, to extend the theoretical insights of the classical theorists, and to break new theoretical frontiers.

With respect to race relations, different circumstances have conditioned its history, but the result has been similar. If one had looked at sociology around World War I, he might have predicted that race relations would become a developing field in the next 25 years. The Negroes' problems were emerging from their "insulated" status in the rural South. Two decades of northward migration, which had accelerated during and after the war, and the occurrence of ugly urban riots in Chicago, East St. Louis, and other cities gave ample evidence that racial problems were going to be visible and serious for a long time to come.

Yet events proved that plausible prediction wrong during the 1920's, 1930's, and 1940's. Sociology became very much preoccupied with "science" and the "scientific method" as it experienced the dominance of a radical positivism in the 1920's and 1930's, the revitalization of interest in systematic theory in the 1930's and 1940's, and the growth of improved methods of empirical research throughout these decades. Correspondingly, it became increasingly "unscientific" and therefore unfashionable to study social problems and "applied" fields such as race relations. Aside from a few pioneering professors at the University of Chicago and their students at other universities, little research was conducted on race and ethnic relations during the interwar period and through the 1940's.

Several other diverse influences also inhibited the rise of the scientific sociological study of race relations. First, the field was virtually without financial support through the 1940's, though this was true of almost every other field of sociology. When support of the behavioral and social sciences began in earnest in the 1950's, race relations was not among the favored fields. Most of the research support of any magnitude emanated from concerns with national defense and health. This decade also witnessed a certain general reluctance on the part of funding agencies to extend support to the study of race, very likely because of the political touchiness of the topic. Some support for the study of ethnic relations came from the Anti-Defamation League, but most of this was concentrated on the study of anti-Semitism, a subject brought brutally to the world's attention by the Nazi regime and World War II.

Second, there was a tendency to regard the study of race relations in terms of racial prejudice and other racial attitudes, thus diverting attention from the systematic analysis of social-structural aspects of the subject. Perhaps this was a by-product of the particular liberal mentality of the 1930's and 1940's, a mentality that tended to deny individual, social, and cultural differences between the races, and to view the cure of racial problems mainly in terms of a cure of whites' illiberal attitudes. There were quite a few descriptive studies during the period (for example, Negroes and labor, churches, housing, medicine, and so on), but these did little to raise the low status of the field of race relations, since they were characterized as non-theoretical and methodologically "soft."

In the 1960's the picture has changed abruptly and radically. The problems of the Negro American have thrust themselves dramatically into the public consciousness. The great dispersion of the Negro population, the growth of urban ghettos, the significant advances of the civil rights movement in the 1950's and the 1960's, and the turbulent racial violence of the late 1960's—all have awakened American citizens and have forewarned them that racial issues will remain among the nation's most serious social problems for many years. Correspondingly, the interest of citizens, policy makers, and social scientists alike in race relations have quickened dramatically. In a state of crisis, the nation is alarmed, confused, and searching desperately for answers.

Under these circumstances, concerned citizens and policy makers have turned to sociologists and other social scientists to supply—and supply quickly—relevant facts, theories and policy guidance. Governmental and private funding agencies have opened their coffers, and, as a result, sponsored research on poverty and race relations has burgeoned to join crime and mental health as one of the most heavily supported areas of study. Government agencies concerned with issues of poverty and race have called on sociologists as expert consultants; municipal governments and social work agencies have done likewise; and the press turns to sociologists more and more for public statements on the nation's racial crisis. And finally, sociologists themselves, as concerned citizens and scholars, have turned their attention increasingly to the study of racial topics in the past few years.

What have these several developments meant for race relations as a scientific field of sociology? In one sense the crisis of the 1960's is beneficial to the field, because both the number of interested sociologists and the level of support for their research have increased rapidly. Yet because of the very urgency accompanying the crisis, race relations stands in some danger of suffering as a scientific enterprise. Under tremendous demand—and with great desire—for quick and specific solutions, sociologists are tempted to conduct their research on short-term, pressing problems; to venture advice without scientific foundation; to suggest policies without adequate factual basis. Necessary as this applied and short-term emphasis is, it may at the same time discourage social scientists from undertaking basic theoretical and methodological studies, as well as careful empirical research on minorities both within and outside the United States. These studies, in addition to the problem-oriented ones, are essential to achieve a more substantial understanding of the conditions of racial conflict and racial harmony.

The following conclusions might be drawn from these reflections. Scientific inquiry will not flourish under conditions of indifference within the profession; and it will not likely flourish if it is starved from lack of support outside the profession. The history of the sociology of religion and much of the history of the sociology of race relations bear out these generalizations. However, neither will scientific inquiry be likely to flourish in an atmosphere of crisis and an interest in quick solution for complex social problems or if it is simply force-fed by crash programs of support. The recent history of the sociology of race relations seems to bear this out. The optimum combination for scientific advance is both a high level of interest in an area among sociologists, and ample support for research, a portion of which is ventured for basic research, conducted without regard for immediate solutions.

# 3
# THE DEVELOPMENT OF SOCIOLOGY AS AN ACADEMIC DISCIPLINE

The history of sociology is unique among all the behavioral and social sciences. Though its roots are in European social thought, it arose first and fastest as an empirical discipline and academic subject in the United States. Furthermore, we have maintained that position of leadership despite the fact that sociology has shown vigorous growth throughout the world in the past two decades.

## EARLY GROWTH

The earliest departments of sociology were founded in this country in the 1890's. At the beginning the discipline was closely linked to the impulse to ameliorate social problems emanating from immigration, race relations, poverty, and crime. In fact the growth of sociology was probably greatly facilitated by the circumstance that America was a nation of immigrants, that group differences based on ethnic and racial variations were obvious, and that America was under great pressure to socialize millions of people reared in other cultures. The department of sociology at the University of Chicago, which dominated the field from the 1890's through World War II, was best known as a center of urban sociology. Using Chicago as a laboratory, both faculty and students produced many books dealing with the pathologies of a heterogeneous urban civilization—crime, juvenile delinquency, unadjusted youth, problems of the family, and the behavior of immigrants.

During the 1930's the emphasis on social problems shifted, as many scholars dealt with unemployment, class conflict, and other issues raised by the great depression. In the 1940's and 1950's many of the leading sociologists turned away from emphasis on social problems and dedicated themselves to theoretical and methodological preoccupations. In many respects these preoccupations still dominate the field. But in the 1960's, sociology has once again been infused with political and social issues arising from the nation's crises of crime, poverty, race relations, education, and mental illness. As we have suggested, sociology's proximity to the public's concern with social problems has not always been conducive to its growth as a scientific discipline. But its history reveals that it has always been in large degree a barometer of the dominant political, social, and intellectual currents of the larger society.

Another factor fostering the growth of sociology in the United States was its unique system of academic organization. In Europe the traditionally self-governing faculties were reluctant to recognize the need to create new disciplines. Many European sociologists held chairs that were not assigned to sociology—Max Weber (1864–1920) was in the economics faculty; Vilfredo Pareto (1848–1923) first achieved eminence as an economist; and Émile Durkheim (1858–1917) and Karl Mannheim (1893–1947) held pedagogical chairs. In American universities, by contrast, administrations and faculties frequently had the power to create new departments in a relatively free way.

The early growth of sociology in South Africa was related to that country's special concerns with race relations, and to the fact that its universities were created after the rise of sociology. In Japan, too, no universities in the Western sense existed until after the Meiji Restoration. As part of their effort to modernize, the Japanese established a large number of private and public universities with the assistance of foreign scholars. Since the new system was not committed to given disciplines, it was easy to introduce new subjects such as sociology into the curriculum. Latin America was the one other area with many sociologists before 1940. Because of Latin America's traditional intellectual orientation toward France and because of the especially great influence of Auguste Comte (1798–1857), most professors who called themselves sociologists in these countries were basically social philosophers. Most of their works were speculative, dealing with the nature of man, society, and the state.

## RECENT TRENDS

After World War II, however, this picture began to change drastically. America has continued to be the center, where sociologists throughout the world look for leadership in the scientific aspects of the discipline. But other countries are moving ahead. In the reformist spirit of the immediate postwar years in France, the government established a number of institutes in the social sciences at the level of the institutes in the natural sciences. Several sociological institutes were founded in Paris, drawing government funds and employing many full-time investigators. Many of France's prominent sociologists began their careers in these institutes. The French universities, however, have been more conservative. The Sorbonne still has only one chair officially assigned to sociology, though other sociologists hold chairs designated as social psychology or social philosophy. The first effort in France to create the equivalent of a sociology department with four professorships has been in the new University of Nanterre.

Sociology has also spread in Scandinavia, where it had a limited academic existence before the war. By now chairs in sociology exist in all Scandinavian universities, although most have only one major position. The advance of sociology in Scandinavia has probably been facilitated by the traditional concern of the Scandinavian nations with questions of social welfare; by the excellent record-keeping of official agencies, which produce first-rate sociological data; and by the widespread knowledge of English as a second language in Scandinavia.

Germany, the home of many classical sociologists, still resists the large-scale development of sociology. The discipline exists as a major subject in only four universities, and two of these—the Free University of Berlin and the University of Constance—were created after World War II. Cologne had been a center of sociology in pre-Hitler Germany under the leadership of Leopold von Wiese. After the war he returned and was able to widen the scope of the discipline. Sociology at Frankfurt has developed largely under the aegis of the Institute for Social Research, established by private financing before the war. The Institute was able to revive after the war and has sponsored much research. Despite the generally conservative picture in post-war Germany, however, the American impact has contributed to the spread of sociology, and most German universities now have at least one chair in sociology.

British sociology adds still another dimension to the historical picture. Before World War II, Britain excelled in anthropology, which had emerged mainly as a study of the non-white societies of the British empire. In Britain itself, sociological inquiry was largely confined to studies of the poor, and was conducted either by sophisticated amateurs or under the aegis of people in social administration (the closest British equivalent to social work). The one major sociology department—in the London School of Economics—was founded before World War I to spur social reform. After 1945, however, the increased concern with egalitarian matters linked to the welfare state led to a corresponding quickening of interest in sociology. In the late 1950's and the 1960's sociology has achieved a major advance. Oxford and Cambridge have both created a number of positions for sociologists. Almost all the older provincial universities and all the new universities in Britain have also set up chairs and departments. Because of the explosive growth, Britain now faces the need to fill many academic positions with high-quality senior sociologists, who, in fact, do not exist.

The spread of sociology in Britain has been paralleled by a growth in Canada, Australia, and New Zealand. Canada had traditionally resisted sociology until the past two decades, despite its close link with American academic life. McGill was the only English-language university with a full department of sociology before World War II; the University of Toronto had a small sociology group as a part of the Department of Political Economy. Laval University was the first supporter of the discipline in French Canada, and the University of Montreal delayed its entry until the 1950's. Today, however, almost every Canadian university has a substantial department. Canada, too, has had a serious recruiting problem, but it has been able to draw in some measure upon both American and Canadian scholars trained in the United States to staff its departments. Australia and New Zealand resisted sociology completely until after World War II, but since that time the discipline has enjoyed a small but steady growth in those countries.

So pervasive has been the post-war spread of sociology that it has now gained a foothold in various authoritarian systems—Poland, Czechoslovakia, Yugoslavia, the Soviet Union, and Spain—where the field had long been politically unacceptable. The Communist countries had been hostile to sociology since the 1920's, when the subject was banned in the Soviet Union as a bourgeois subject, opposed to Marxist historical materialism. Efforts to revive the prewar sociology—which was largely speculative in character—in Eastern Europe were suppressed around 1950, when the Stalinist regimes assumed power in all these states, except Yugoslavia. With the de-Stalinization in the mid-fifties, sociology emerged as an acceptable if not completely legitimate body of thought, and it took the form mainly as a set of methods to inquire into social problems facing some of the eastern European countries. In part because it had been banned by the Stalinist regimes, sociology became very popular among many young faculty and students as an alternative to Marxist rigidities. Poland was the first country to create a full and vigorous discipline, including departments at many universities and large institutes set up as sections of the Academy of Science. Many Polish sociologists were enabled to spend a year in the United States under the aegis of the Ford Foundation. As a result of these kinds of contacts the discipline absorbed many American approaches.

Sociology has developed as a major field in Yugoslavia as well. The relaxation of dictatorial controls in Hungary also resulted in a flowering of the discipline. Recently Czechoslovakian sociology took the lead in Eastern Europe, mainly as a result of the emergence of a liberal political regime, though the Soviet intervention into the internal affairs in the summer of 1968 cast a great cloud over the future of free inquiry in that land. Sociology in Poland has also suffered periodic setbacks, with some of its leaders being suspended from their academic positions after the triumph of authoritarian and anti-Semitic elements within the Polish Communist Party.

In the Soviet Union itself sociology has recently experienced a rapid growth. In the past few years a number of sociological institutes have been set up in different parts of the country, and a few chairs have been established. The field is clearly still suspect, but no longer regarded as illegitimate. The Soviet Sociological Association numbers more than 1,000 members. The regime often turns to sociologists for research on various social problems in areas such as labor productivity, education, crime, and alcoholism. In general, the attitudes of Communist political leaders toward sociology appear to be ambivalent; they have learned that sociological techniques of inquiry can provide useful information, but at the same time they seek to prevent it from dealing with theories that may question the premises of Marxist thought.

In Spain also, the gradual erosion of the authoritarian regime has opened the door for sociology. Sociological studies of industrial efficiency and social mobility have demonstrated their value to the political and economic elites. Both academic chairs and private institutes have sprung up around the country. As in the Communist world, however, sociology has proven to be a potentially disturbing field to the Spanish authorities. Sociologists and their students have been in the forefront of criticism of the regime and its ideology. In a number of authoritarian countries, therefore, sociology has been allowed to become somewhat more free because it has been found to be useful. At the same time it is always a source of uneasiness, and a target for harmful political interventions, because a freely developing sociology almost inevitably poses questions that regimes do not want to hear.

Sociology has experienced great vitality beyond the European continent. In Japan, most of the nearly 500 institutions of higher learning have sociology departments. As a result, Japan has more academic sociologists than any country except the United States. Japanese scholarship, moreover, is very much in the mainstream of Western sociology. Practically every Japanese sociologist reads English or another Western language, and much research of good quality is conducted. Unfortunately, few Westerners read Japanese, and little Japanese research is translated into Western languages. Because of this gap in communications, sociology as a world discipline has benefited too little from the extensive work of the Japanese.

Latin American sociology is still dominated by the tradition of social philosophy and speculative inquiry, but the situation is currently changing, as sociologists trained in empirical research are beginning to appear. Serious empirical scholarship is constricted by the lack of research funds, and by the fact that most Latin American faculty are still part-time and ill-paid professors, and must secure much of their livelihood in law, business, civil service, and elsewhere. During the past ten years, however, the situation has improved as the number of full-time academic posts has increased and as a number of research institutes—often financed with North American money—have been established. A substantial number of Latin American sociologists have been receiving their training in the United States or France, and others are trained in institutes like Educational Film Institute for Latin America, a training center established under the auspices of United Nations Educational, Scientific, and Cultural Organization in Santiago.

By far the most serious obstacle to the emergence of academic sociology in Latin America is the menace of political instability. Sociology has had an especially creative growth in Argentina and Brazil, but this has been reversed as a result of military coups in both countries. A number of the best scholars have been forced from their university positions. Some have been able to continue their work abroad, however, or in non-university-connected institutes in their home countries.

Modern sociology has also emerged in other parts of the "third world." Perhaps the most important center has been Israel, which has strong departments at several universities. A number of African universities have departments of sociology, and the discipline is recognized as an important subject in many Asian countries, particularly the Philippines, India, Indonesia, and Pakistan.

Clearly, sociology's effort to establish itself as a recognized field in the universities of the world is now over. It is firmly located in many countries, and gaining at least a tenuous foothold in many others. Increasingly, both government and industry draw upon sociologists to study major social problems. In the underdeveloped countries, the field focuses, understandably, on problems of economic development and village life. In societies with many racial, ethnic, or linguistic groups, sociologists are increasingly called upon as experts to deal with problems resulting from inter-group tensions. Demographers are becoming more influential with respect to national and international population policies. Crime and delinquency have also been acknowledged as social concerns to which sociology can contribute policy recommendations.

And finally, the policy relevance of sociology has been enhanced by the growing concern in many countries with the "culture of poverty" and the social mobility of individuals reared in "culturally deprived" circumstances. Because the social problems are so enormous, and because sociology cannot provide definite answers in many cases, the traffic flowing across the bridge between academic sociology and public policy is still very light in most places in the world. But, at least, the bridge has been built.

# 4
# SOCIOLOGY AND ITS APPLICATIONS

## THE PRACTICAL IMPORTANCE OF SOCIOLOGY

If we were to list the subfields in sociology in one column, and the social evils and social problems that burden contemporary American society in another, we would discover a remarkable correspondence between the two columns. Corresponding to the subfield of "race and ethnic relations" we would find the persistence of racial prejudice and discrimination, the crises of the black ghettos, and the plight of Mexican-Americans and Puerto Rican migrants. Corresponding to "deviance" we would find crime, delinquency, and drug abuse. Corresponding to "family and socialization" we would find divorce, generational conflict, and mental illness. Corresponding to "collective behavior" we would find the problems of widespread malaise, protest, and disruptive violence. For "sociology of education," "sociology of conflict," "social stratification," and the rest we would find equally close correspondence.

It is clear, then, that sociology has relevance for the vast range of social and political problems that beset a complex, heterogeneous, and dynamic society. It is equally clear that the sociologist has become much more publicly involved in these problems in the past decade than ever before. Sociologists are being hired in greater numbers by government agencies, businesses, hospitals, and other organizations.

116

They are summoned more frequently for consultation on vital public issues. And they find themselves quoted more often in the public media as experts on one issue or another. Not so clear, however, is the exact character of the sociologist's expanded role in the larger society—what it is and what it should be.

Sociologists themselves are divided on such questions, as are people in almost every other discipline. Some are basically indifferent to the applications of the field to contemporary policy issues, and are concerned mainly with the methodological and theoretical advance of the field as a science. Others are primarily interested in the applications of sociology to social problems and public efforts to improve society. A third and very vocal group argues that sociologists are morally obligated to speak out as critics of the larger society, and that they should use their professional positions and their special talents to effect radical social change. This group is openly hostile both to "the scientific establishment," which is in effect, they feel, endorsing the *status quo* by non-involvement, and to applied sociologists who are content to work within the existing structure of society.

Because of this diversity of viewpoints within the profession, much of the public discussion of sociology's ethical and policy implications is clouded by preconceptions of *the* role of the sociologist in larger society. Actually, the sociologist has a variety of possible roles, which should be distinguished clearly from one another. The sociologist may be regarded, for example, as a person with special expertise or special knowledge that places him in a unique position to predict the consequences of social arrangements, social policies, and social programs. Another interpretation views him as a person with a special claim to knowledge that should legitimize public policy. Or he may be viewed, along with other professionals, as a person of special status and influence in the community. And, finally, he may be regarded as a citizen who should be especially concerned with public policies. Discussion should follow different lines, depending on which of these possible roles is being considered; but, as we said, too often the various roles are lumped indistinguishably into one, and discussion necessarily becomes confused because it shoots off into so many directions at once.

Our own view is that it is mainly in the role of a person with special expertise that the sociologists, *qua* sociologists, can lay legitimate claim to having a unique or special relation to the larger society. We believe that the sociologist generates a certain type of findings, and has a certain type of theoretical perspective that can and should be taken into account by policy-makers and decision-makers. As such the sociologist can legitimately inform and influence public policy. He can, for example, point up some of the social consequences, benefits, and costs of different types of programs for school integration on the basis of his general knowledge and his specific findings; and he can further point out some of the social benefits and sociological complications that may be expected to arise from the "maximum feasible participation of the poor" in action programs designed to relieve unemployment and poverty.

It is not appropriate, however, to press this argument to its extreme, and to suggest that sociologists are uniquely qualified to hold high positions of policy responsibility—to be "sociologist kings," as it were—or to be in any sense the moral guardians of any particular public policy. The qualifications and responsibilities of the policy-maker are both diffuse and diverse; and technical training in social science is no guarantee of effectiveness as a policy-maker. Furthermore, the justification for public policy cannot be derived solely from social-scientific considerations. For instance, the policy of integrating the races in educational institutions must be legitimized above all on *moral* grounds— on grounds that it is morally wrong to deprive any group of the benefits of society because of racial characteristics—not on the basis of some special sociological insights. Sociologists do, however, have something special to say on the likely costs and consequences of failing to integrate, integrating slowly, or integrating rapidly. Finally, we maintain that nothing in the sociologist's professional status either permits or obliges him to be more concerned with civic issues than any other citizen. The rights and responsibilities of citizenship rest on an individual's membership in the polity of the nation, not on the possession of a specialized knowledge or expertise.

## CONTRIBUTIONS TO POLICY

What are the ways in which sociological knowledge has actually articulated with practical action—whether this be in business organizations, professional life, or governmental policy? Sociology has contributed in a number of different ways, and with varying degrees of effectiveness:

First, sociologists have supplied facts or findings for rather specific policy purposes. The most obvious examples come from assignments undertaken by sociologists for the military in World War II, in which they conducted investigations of the effect of bombing on the morale of enemy populations, studied the effects of psychological welfare, and developed the "point system" by which priorities for discharge were determined during the period of demobilization. To choose a more recent and contrasting example, the multitude of statistics concerning the extent and effects of segregation in the nation's schools contained in the "Coleman Report" (*Equality of Educational Opportunity*, 1966) were gathered specifically for the President and Congress in accord with congressional legislation. Most often these facts and findings are supplied within the context of already-determined policies, but the input of unanticipated facts may also generate new policies or turn existing policies in new directions.

Second, policy-makers may be alerted to the "sociological way of thinking," either through direct consultation with sociologists or through acquaintance with the sociological perspective. In this instance specific facts are not applied to specific policy problems. Acquaintance with "the sociological way of thinking" serves to sensitize policy-makers to unexpected facts and problems and to shape their decisions, but it is rarely determinate enough that specific policies may be derived from it. Consider only two examples of the importance of the sociological approach. Academic administrators who have recently decided to increase the admissions of minority-group students would be well advised to acquaint themselves with the kinds of consequences that arise when a group's expectations are rising rapidly; with the importance of reference-group theory; and with the ambivalences that arise when any group moves from one cultural context to another. To choose another example, the President's Advisory Commission on Civil Disorders—upon being asked "Why did the riots of the summer of 1967 happen?"—called extensively on sociologists for consultation. Sociologists were not able to give specific findings and explanations, but they were able to call to the Commission's attention unsuspected sources of civil disturbance

and its control that could not be ignored in the search for an explanation. We should add, by way of caution, that sociologists differ among
themselves in conceiving the exact nature of "the sociological way of
thinking"; thus policy-makers may well receive a variety of lines of
advice, all in the name of "the sociological approach."

Sometimes, however, carefully conducted sociological research contains more precise suggestions as to specific lines of policy than might
emerge from a general sociological perspective. For example, research
on high school students has revealed that the educational aspirations
of students from different social classes are influenced by the dominant-
social-class character of a high school. Thus, students from a working-
class background enrolled in a predominantly high-status school have
a significantly higher level of aspiration than those enrolled in a low-
status school; and the sons of professionals in a high-status school have
significantly higher aspirations than those in a low-status school. While
such findings are not definitive, and while many other factors than the
dominant-class character of a school affect aspirations, these findings
are of direct relevance to boards of education whose policy decisions
affect the social-class composition of high schools in their districts.

Third, specific sociological theories may be applied to obtain specific
results. The parallel here is from economic theory, on the basis of which
rather specific solutions and predictions of the impact of policy changes
on monetary or fiscal policy can be generated by applying abstract
principles that relate a number of general economic variables. The predictions of the impact of a tax hike or an increase in the interest rate,
for example, are grounded in price theory, the theory of the firm, and
the theory of the household. By and large, sociological theory is not
sufficiently precise in its formulation to permit these kinds of predictions,
except in such subfields as demography. In most areas policy-makers
must rely on qualitative estimates with varying degrees of reliability.

Fourth, sociological methods may be used in a variety of organizational settings other than the academic. Business and marketing enterprises, for example, engage in extensive market research, relying mainly
on survey methods that have been developed and employed by sociologists and other social scientists. The poll has become a favorite instru-
ment of the press, political candidates, and political parties.

Finally, the sociologist himself often is employed for purposes of research and analysis in some agency other than a college or university. Many non-academic sociologists find employment in government agencies—particularly the Bureau of the Census and the Department of Health, Education, and Welfare. However, as can be seen in Table 5-2, Chapter 5, their numbers are small in comparison to economists and psychologists in the civil service. Other sociologists are finding employment in increasing numbers in business firms, hospitals, and welfare agencies.

In singling out these several sociological contributions to policy, we must not lose sight of the fact that most policy problems are interdisciplinary ones, and that the insights of many disciplines must be brought to bear on policies and decisions. Contemporary social life is so complex that its problems cannot be solved by academic specialists who bring their respective bits of knowledge separately to bear on them. To choose an obvious example, one cannot contemplate the multitude of problems facing our urban centers for long without concluding that they are simultaneously economic, political, ecological, social, psychological, and medical in nature. As men of action attempt to come to grips with these problems, they find that these many aspects cannot be separated from one another. Furthermore, because of these interconnections, any effort to apply resources to the solution of any one problem is bound to have varying consequences. To introduce a large housing project into the center of a large city, for example, generates profound repercussions on the employment, political participation, neighborhood structure, and the ethnic relations of its inhabitants. Unless these repercussions are known and taken into account, social policy is likely to be deflected or even subverted by unanticipated consequences. Adequate knowledge of the repercussions, moreover, depends on the simultaneous application of principles from many specialized disciplines, and the collaboration of many specialists. The complexity of applying knowledge to social life, then, argues for establishing advisory and consultative bodies on an interdisciplinary basis, so that the principles of the various behavioral and social sciences may be linked as they are applied to the social world.

## Points of Tension and Conflict

The flow of knowledge from sociology to the rest of society is not always without conflicts, tensions, and ethical problems. Moreover, most of the "sore spots" do not involve simply matters of right and wrong—on either side of the exchange—but reflect unresolved difficulties that resist unqualified resolution. Hence we can expect that they will be with us in the foreseeable future.

The first point of tension between sociology and the larger society arises from the fact that sociologists necessarily study and make public some things that many people would prefer to keep in the social closet, as it were. By virtue of their professional commitments, sociologists—like anthropologists and psychologists—must ask objective questions about many sacred, taboo, or taken-for-granted subjects, such as intimate family relations, sex, and religious conviction. They also uncover social problems that many people do not like to think about—widespread poverty, for example, or widespread drug usage among youth. Furthermore, any sociologist who reveals the ideological rationalizations of a governing regime, an interest group, or a social movement is bound to be unpopular with those he is studying.

In studying unpopular or undercover activities, the sociologist is faced with a number of difficult and perennial ethical and technical problems: How can he provide safeguards to protect the anonymity of informants? How can the conflicting claims of personal privacy and the professional sociologist's interest in getting the facts be reconciled? To what degree is confidential information obtained by the research sociologist privileged? To what extent is the sociologist obliged to report breaches of the law to the authorities when he discovers them? To what degree is the sociologist subtly "seduced" into either endorsing or debunking the values or motives of those he is studying? No definitive answers to these thorny questions have been devised as yet. They will probably emerge as a result of the evolution of a better research methodology and a system of professional ethics, and perhaps also as a result of administrative and court decisions.

A second point of tension between sociology and the larger society arises from the fact that policy-makers and others often demand answers that sociologists do not have. In fact, a great gulf exists between the array of pressing social problems—crime, delinquency, violence, racial inequalities, war and conflict, for example—and the sociological knowledge that is relevant to their solution. This gulf is likely to lead to two unfortunate sets of consequences. On the one hand the sociologist, cognizant of the limitations of his theories and findings, will decline to provide advice at all, thus disappointing the policy-maker and perhaps isolating himself in the future. On the other hand, the sociologist, under pressure to come up with answers, may "oversell" his "product" and give unfounded or premature advice that may subsequently disillusion those who have relied on it. Ideally the best course of action—indeed the obligation—for the sociologist is to advise as competently and honestly as his capabilities permit, and to reveal his ignorance as readily as his insights. But when under great pressure for solutions, it is difficult for him to tread the narrow path between excessive timidity and excessive definitiveness.

A third and related point of tension arises from the fact that policy-makers and others interested in social action seek advice on factors that will *produce* change, whereas sociologists in their general search for basic social forces at work, are likely to stress many factors that will *prevent* or *inhibit* change. The businessman, interested in improving productivity, for example, may turn to the sociologist for insights about ways to change the social organization of his plant to this end. The sociologist may respond by pointing out the crucial role of the informal work group in worker productivity. Such advice is frustrating to the businessman, because these kinds of primary group relations are among the most difficult to modify by company policy. Or the school administrator may be interested in tailoring his high school's educational program to minimize drop-out rates; the consulting sociologist may point out to him—correctly—that the most important determinants for continuing in high school are found in the family structure, ethnic-group membership, and social-class position of the students. All these are beyond the control of the educational administrator, and, for that matter, generally difficult to influence by legislative or social-action programs. Much of the subject-matter of sociology, in fact, deals with those very institutions that are often highly resistant to change. There is more than a grain of truth in the policy-maker's complaint that, whenever he calls on a sociologist to tell him how to make a program work, the sociologist tells him a dozen ways in which it is bound to fail.

A fourth point of tension arises when we consider the different professional perspectives of a sociologist—or any social scientist, for that matter—and a person responsible for making decisions in some organizational context. The parole officer, for example, wants to know whether a given individual will be re-incarcerated while on parole; the sociologist is interested in generating statements of regularity regarding the rate of recidivism among parolees by systematically investigating different social and psychological variables. The parole officer wants to make the best prediction he can about a *specific* outcome, whereas the sociologist can give him only *general* statements about relevant factors. To put the matter more generally, the decision-maker's main responsibility is to apply knowledge to concrete organizational or professional goals in an uncontrolled or partially controlled setting; the sociologist's main professional responsibility is to address himself to problems in a scientific or quasi-scientific framework. Because the two are directing themselves to different kinds of problems, the knowledge generated by the one cannot be translated into certain decisions by the other. While the sociologist's findings are obviously helpful to the decision-maker in a general way, a residue of uncertainty, frustration, and perhaps conflict is virtually bound to remain.

A fifth point of tension concerns the differences in institutional values and loyalties of sociologists and of those responsible for decisions. By and large the professional sociologist has a strong loyalty to the tradition of scientific and humanistic learning as institutionalized in centers of higher education. Those who seek his knowledge or counsel are almost always in some other kind of organizational setting (a business firm, for instance) and for that reason have loyalties to other types of values (the ethic of profit-maximization, for instance). This circumstance tends to generate difficulties of communication and perhaps conflicts of value between the two. And the sociologist who takes employment in an organization other than a college or university may experience feelings that he has fallen in status or even "sold out" or otherwise deserted his academic calling.

A sixth point of tension arises from the fact that the sociologist is viewed only partly as an "expert." A policy-maker will readily acknowledge that the chemist or the economist is an expert in a certain body of knowledge, and possesses information and techniques that are unknown to him. The same value is not always applied to the sociologist. This is due in part to the fact that sociology is, in fact, not as developed scientifically as some other disciplines. But another factor is also pertinent. In some measure, every man is his own sociologist. He has his social truths, his social faiths, and his views about how society operates. He is apt to feel very strongly about things—family, religion, politics—that sociologists attempt to study dispassionately. As a result, sociological advice, even when well-founded, is likely to encounter delicate sensitivities and ideologies. This circumstance is likely to generate argumentation rather than communication, conflict rather than cooperation.

These tensions, while considerable, are also reducible. One means of reducing them lies in improving our understanding of the conditions under which sociological and other knowledge is in fact effective in guiding policy, and the conditions under which it is not. This is a legitimate and important area of social research, to which social and behavioral scientists could profitably devote more attention. If they conducted this research in collaboration with policy-makers, perhaps on temporary leave from their posts, the results would probably be even more informative. Another way of reducing the tensions would be to establish advisory and consultative relations between social and behavioral scientists and governmental agencies on a more continuous basis than at present. Standing or revolving advisory panels of social and behavioral scientists are better able than *ad hoc* advisory groups to acquaint themselves with the policy concerns of the respective agencies and are consequently able to contribute theories, findings, and advice on a more informed basis. Continuous interaction with behavioral and social scientists would also permit policy-makers to acquaint themselves with the content and style of social-scientific thinking, and to make more realistic their expectations of what behavioral and social scientists can and can not contribute.

Finally, we must say a word about the well-worn subject of the use of sociological knowledge for purposes of social or political manipulation. Ever since knowledge about human beings began to be developed, it has been accompanied by the fear that it can be used to manipulate people for social and political purposes, and to render them help-less by controlling their behavior. We agree that all knowledge—including sociological knowledge—is a means of power and can be brought to bear on the control of the social environment. But we must deny that sociological knowledge leads, by definition, to manipula-tion, exploitation, or subjugation. Knowledge, like all means of power, can be used for good or ill. People do not complain when knowledge is used in the manipulation of social arrangements for good purposes. Al-most nobody objects to campaigns of social indoctrination designed to induce people to take advantage of a vaccine that will prevent a dread disease. Most people do not object when we create sociologically viable arrangements to ensure the success of a program of racial integration in the schools or to assure that persons from modest backgrounds are given maximum educational opportunities. Surely, however, all these are examples of manipulation—that is, manipulation for what most people think are good purposes. The menace of manipulation arises only when knowledge is applied for questionable or illegitimate pur-poses or when the purposes are unclear, hidden, or disguised. The soci-ologist as scientist and citizen is obliged not to use his knowledge to manipulate those whom he studies and he is obliged to speak out when he senses the danger that sociological knowledge may be put to illegiti-mate purposes. The ultimate purposes to which knowledge is actually put, however, is a matter to be determined not by the creators of the knowledge but rather by men in their capacity as citizens of the polity.

# 5
# MANPOWER AND
# RESOURCES IN
# SOCIOLOGY

At this point we conclude our substantive account of sociology. We have tried to portray its diversity, vitality, and excitement. We have tried to give a balanced assessment of its strengths and weaknesses, its intellectual accomplishments and needs, its promises and problems. And we have tried to illustrate its relevance for the problems faced by society.

As we have described sociology as an intellectual endeavor, a number of implicit recommendations have emerged. For example, in commenting on the strengths and weaknesses of the data base for the discipline's various fields, we were implicitly recommending measures to sustain or improve this base. In assessing the conceptual status of these fields, we were implicitly recommending measures to sustain the theoretical position of the stronger ones and to advance that of the weaker ones. And in discussing the consequences of different patterns of financial and organizational support for sociology, we were simultaneously developing some suggestions about the pattern of that support.

We shall make these recommendations as explicit as possible in Chapter 6. These recommendations flow mainly from our assessment of sociology as a discipline. But in addition, the recommendations must take account of the fundamental fact that sociology is a body of ideas that is created, sustained, and transmitted by professionals in social institutions —in colleges and universities, research institutes, and agencies that address social problems. Our recommendations therefore deal in part with

**127**

fostering the optimum institutional arrangements for teaching and re-search in sociology.

As a prelude to formulating the recommendations, then, we shall describe sociology in terms of its manpower, the allocation of its personnel, its capacity to educate students and train future professionals, and its patterns of financial support. In many respects sociology is experiencing the same problems associated with rapid growth that are being faced by the other behavioral and social sciences. It does, however, have a few problems of its own; we shall dwell principally on these.

In one sense this task is an unwelcome one, because the data on topics like the research interests of sociologists, the sources of their support, and the distribution of their time among various professional activities are often not available in reliable form. In many cases we shall have to speculate on the basis of limited data. The main sources we have been able to use are the data collected by the Behavioral and Social Sciences Department Survey;[1] data collected by governmental and other agencies; past surveys of sociologists and sociology departments; and our own first-hand knowledge of the field, acquired as practicing professionals.

## HOW MANY SOCIOLOGISTS?

The magnitude of an intellectual discipline can be measured in a variety of ways. Most of our report has attempted to delineate the scope and dimensions of the intellectual activities pursued by professional sociologists; presently we shall inquire into the size of its output of educated and trained personnel. For the moment, however, let us view sociology in terms of the numbers of sociologists who affiliate themselves with its central professional body, the American Sociological Association.

The membership of the American Sociological Association numbered 12,300 in 1968. In numbers, sociology is less than half the size of

[1] The questionnaire survey of universities is described in *The Behavioral and Social Sciences: Outlook and Needs* (Englewood Cliffs, N.J.: Prentice-Hall, Inc., 1969), Appendix. In some of the tables that follow, reference is made to the Departmental Questionnaire, which was part of the Survey. The sociology departments included in the Survey are listed in an appendix to this report.

psychology; smaller than history, economics, and political science; somewhat larger than anthropology; and about double the size of geography. The size of the membership, however, exaggerates the number of professional sociologists. Anyone who is interested in sociology and willing to pay annual dues may become an Associate Member of the Association. As a result, many social workers, nurses, educators, state officials, and other behavioral and social scientists become members. In addition, there are several thousand Student Members. The categories of Active Members and Fellows, which may be used to denote the professional sociologists, include about 4,500 members. We are struck by the fact that the intellectual activities of sociology are almost unlimited in scope and diversity, which our report has documented, and, in the face of this fact, its manpower is relatively limited.

Sociology has only very recently attained its present size. In 1935 the Association enjoyed a total membership of only 1,169—scarcely large or anonymous enough to call for name-tags at the annual meetings. By 1945 the figure was 1,309. In the next decade, however, the membership more than tripled, to 4,454, and between 1955 and 1965 it almost doubled again, to 8,892. As the other panel reports document, all the behavioral and social sciences have shared in greater or less degree in this explosive surge of growth and interest since World War II.

## WHERE DO SOCIOLOGISTS WORK?

As we have noted, a great majority of all PhD sociologists find their principal employment in educational institutions and the remainder are scattered through federal government, other government, non-profit organizations, industry, and business. Close examination of this distribution of personnel leads to the conclusion that the concentration of sociological talent in educational institutions is considerably greater than it is in some of the other behavioral and social sciences.

Table 5-1 shows the relative numbers and percentages of PhD's in psychology, economics, political science, and sociology in different employments. Both psychologists and economists are represented more heavily—both in total numbers and in percentages—in "federal government" and in "business and industry" than are sociologists; psychologists

TABLE 5-1 EMPLOYMENT OF ECONOMISTS, PSYCHOLOGISTS, SOCIOLOGISTS, AND POLITICAL SCIENTISTS HOLDING MA OR PhD AS HIGHEST DEGREE, 1968 (PERCENTILE DISTRIBUTION)

| Type of Employer[a] | Economists MA | Economists PhD | Psychologists MA | Psychologists PhD | Sociologists MA | Sociologists PhD | Political Scientists MA | Political Scientists PhD |
|---|---|---|---|---|---|---|---|---|
| Educational institutions | 46% | 76% | 54% | 60% | 76% | 88% | 71% | 87% |
| Federal government | 17 | 8 | 5 | 7 | 5 | 3 | 9 | 5 |
| State and local governments | 5 | 4 | 14 | 6 | 6 | 1 | 5 | 2 |
| Military | 2 | * | 1 | 1 | 1 | * | 4 | 1 |
| Nonprofit organizations | 5 | 4 | 12 | 10 | 7 | 5 | 5 | 3 |
| Business and industry | 22 | 7 | 9 | 7 | 3 | 1 | 4 | 1 |
| Self-employed | 2 | 1 | 4 | 8 | 1 | 1 | 1 | 1 |
| Other employers | 1 | * | 1 | 1 | 1 | 1 | 1 | * |
| Total | 100% | 100% | 100% | 100% | 100% | 100% | 100% | 100% |
| N | 4,021 | 6,008 | 7,499 | 14,370 | 2,104 | 3,272 | 1,730 | 2,951 |

Source: National Science Foundation, *American Scientific Manpower, 1968*, Appendix Table A-5 (in process). The *National Scientific Register*, from which these data come, is an incomplete and somewhat unrepresentative sample, but gives some impression of patterns of employment.

[a] Excludes "Not employed" and "No report."

* Less than 1 percent.

are represented more heavily in the "self-employment" and "other government" categories than are sociologists. Correspondingly, a greater percentage of PhD sociologists and political scientists find their employment in educational institutions, though not a greater number, since both sociology and political science are smaller than economics and psychology.

If we view the distribution of employment of sociologists according to their levels of training, it becomes apparent that the more highly trained —those with PhDs—are concentrated in educational institutions, whereas those with MA's are more heavily represented in the various applied settings. Within educational institutions, moreover, PhD's are more heavily concentrated than MA's at the universities and four-year colleges. In a survey of the employment of PhD's and MA's in sociology conducted in 1960, 73 percent of the PhD's found employment "on teaching and research staffs of universities and four-year colleges," while the corresponding figure for MA's was 30 percent. On the other hand, 18 percent of the MA's were in "other teaching and educational service" (presumably in junior colleges and high schools), as contrasted with only 5 percent of the PhD's.[2]

One clear implication emerges from these data: As the apparent need for applied sociology is increasing rapidly, the availability of sociologists for applied employments is considerably less than in some other disciplines. Furthermore, those sociologists who are in applied employments generally have less professional training than those in full-time positions in educational institutions.[3] If our estimates of the impending manpower shortage in academic sociology are correct (see below, pp. 142–46), this situation is likely to become even more exaggerated, because of the enormous expected demand for sociologists in institutions of higher learning during the next ten years. This evident and probably increasing discrepancy between the need for applied sociology and the availability of sociological talent underscores the problems associated with the applications of sociology outlined in Chapter 4.

[2] Elbridge Sibley, *The Education of Sociologists in the United States* (New York: Russell Sage Foundation, 1963), p. 56. Data are from Schedules II-B and V of the Sibley survey.

[3] One qualification is in order. About one of ten sociology PhD's in educational institutions is not attached primarily to a department of sociology, but in some more "applied" setting, such as a professional school. *Ibid.*, p. 50.

## EDUCATION IN SOCIOLOGY PRIOR
## TO GRADUATE TRAINING

The functions of undergraduate instruction in sociology are many and diverse—to recruit and offer preliminary training to future professionals, who will complete their work in graduate schools; to provide skills and information for those being trained for work in the applied professions—social work, criminology, and education, for example; and to offer an intellectual perspective that constitutes an important ingredient in any liberal arts program. All of these functions are both necessary and desirable features of undergraduate education in sociology.

Those who teach undergraduate sociology have witnessed a great increase in numbers of their students during the past decade. In 1957, 6,383 bachelor's degrees were granted, 8,183 in 1962, and 17,751 in 1967. In addition, faculties in sociology departments gave courses to many thousands of students not majoring in sociology. This rate of growth promises to continue during the next ten years. According to careful estimates, the methodology of which is reviewed in the general report of the Behavioral and Social Sciences Survey, the number of bachelor's degrees will be 28,300 by 1972, and 49,900 by 1977.[4] Figure 5-1 shows the numerical and percentage increases in both actual and projected bachelor's degrees.

From the standpoint of the future of the profession, this increase is likely to provide a much broader base for recruiting talented young people into graduate training. On the other hand, the present structure of undergraduate teaching in sociology has a number of peculiarities that suggest that its problems of recruiting and training future professionals are, if anything, more serious than in other disciplines. Let us review these peculiarities.

First, those who ultimately become college and university teachers of sociology decide on their areas of specialization very late in their college careers. According to a survey of faculty members conducted in 1963, only 21.5 percent of sociologists had decided on their fields by the end

---

[4] See *The Behavioral and Social Sciences: Outlook and Needs,* Appendix, for a discussion of the methods for projecting degrees.

of their sophomore year. This contrasts with a percentage of 30.1 for political scientists, 31.6 for economists, 44.4 for historians, and a mean for all teaching fields of 51.5.[5] Whatever the reasons, the "late blooming" effect for potential sociologists poses special problems for their

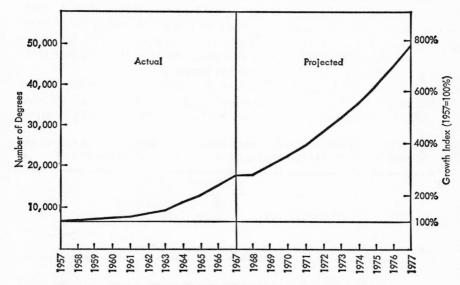

**FIGURE 5-1 SOCIOLOGY BACHELOR'S AND FIRST PROFESSIONAL DEGREES ACTUALLY AWARDED, 1957–67, AND PROJECTED TO 1977**

Source: Office of Education for 1957–67 degrees; *The Behavioral and Social Sciences: Outlook and Needs* (Englewood Cliffs, N.J.: Prentice-Hall, Inc., 1969), Appendix D, for projections 1968–77.

teachers—problems of generating appreciation of and commitment to the sociological perspective, and problems of exposing students to a vast array of sociological ideas, information, and techniques in a relatively short period of time.

Part of the delay in selecting sociology as a field of specialization is based on the fact that sociology courses are offered only infrequently in

[5] Department of Health, Education and Welfare, *Teaching Faculty in Universities and Four-Year Colleges*, Spring, 1963. OE–53022–63, Washington, 1966. Table 15, p. 90.

secondary schools—in contrast to economics and history, for example. These differences may diminish, however, as more high school students begin to take sociology courses. Through programs such as Sociological Resources for Social Studies, supported by the National Science Foundation under the auspices of the American Sociological Association, more high school students are being exposed to sociology earlier in their education. The program is designed to provide increased intellectual stimulation to the student and to encourage him to consider the career possibilities in the field. This and similar programs should affect both the number and quality of students entering the field.

A second peculiarity, beyond late career choice, is that undergraduate training in sociology takes place mainly in departments that do not have graduate training programs. As indicated in Table 5-2, only 25 percent of

**TABLE 5-2  PRODUCTION OF BACHELOR'S DEGREES IN PhD-GRANTING DEPARTMENTS AS PERCENTAGES OF TOTAL DEGREE PRODUCTION**

| Department | AB Degrees (1965–66) | | | |
| | Total Degrees | Granted within PhD Departments | | Order of size |
| | Number | Number[a] | Percentage of Total | |
|---|---|---|---|---|
| Total | 93,482 | 33,674 | 36 | |
| Anthropology | 1,503 | 930 | 62 | 1 |
| Economics | 11,585 | 4,302 | 37 | 4 |
| History | 28,770 | 9,482 | 33 | 5 |
| Political science | 16,620 | 6,634 | 40 | 3 |
| Psychology | 16,966 | 7,158 | 42 | 2 |
| Sociology | 15,203 | 3,868 | 25 | 7 |
| Geography | 1,934 | 592 | 31 | 6 |

Sources: U.S. Office of Education for Column 1; Departmental Questionnaire for Columns 2 and 3.

[a] Adjusted for item non-response and departmental non-response.

the total bachelor's degrees in sociology granted in 1965–66 were within PhD-granting departments, a percentage considerably lower than that of any other behavioral and social science. The implication of this is that initial undergraduate exposure to sociology often occurs in a context in which faculty members are less likely to be involved in research, research facilities are lacking, and interaction with graduate students is not possible—in short, in which professional research and training are not in evidence. This is likely to place sociology at a disadvantage in exposure of undergraduates to professional sociology and recruiting them into it. Even in PhD-granting institutions in which the same faculty members teach both undergraduates and graduates—often in the same classes— the prospects for recruitment are often not propitious. On the basis of his impressionistic survey, Sibley remarked on "the often very large size of classes and the relatively very small number of undergraduates majoring in sociology" in the large universities.[6]

Third, sociology attracts more women than men as undergraduate majors, but this relationship is reversed at the graduate level. Moreover, as Table 5-3 shows, it contrasts in this respect with the behavioral and

**TABLE 5-3   RATIOS OF MEN TO WOMEN IN BA'S, MA'S, AND PhD'S FOR SOCIOLOGY AND FOR TOTAL BEHAVIORAL AND SOCIAL SCIENCES, SELECTED YEARS FOR ENTIRE UNITED STATES ***

| Year | Sociology | | | Total | | |
|------|-----|-----|-----|-----|-----|-----|
| | BA | MA | PhD | BA | MA | PhD |
| 1957 | 0.8 | 1.3 | 7.4 | 2.3 | 3.4 | 8.4 |
| 1962 | 0.8 | 2.7 | 5.7 | 2.1 | 3.4 | 7.1 |
| 1967 | 0.7 | 2.4 | 4.5 | 1.9 | 2.8 | 5.6 |

* Source: U.S. Office of Education.

social sciences in general. The table indicates a general trend toward increasing proportions of women at all levels of advancement, both in sociology and in the totals. But for sociology, the ratio is markedly in favor of women at the BA level, whereas BA's in all the behavioral and social sciences are about two to one in favor of men. At the PhD level, however, the ratio of men to women in sociology was 4.5 in 1967, only slightly lower than for the behavioral and social sciences in general.[7]

[6] Sibley, op. cit., p. 88.
[7] Other evidence shows that women who do pursue graduate work suffer a considerably higher attrition rate than men. According to surveys conducted by Sibley in

Apparently many women who choose sociology as an undergraduate major either do no further work in the field or major in sociology as a preliminary to entering other fields, such as education or social work.

Sociology emerges as a discipline whose potential recruits are exposed to its *professional and social-scientific aspects* less and later than in other behavioral and social sciences. As a result of these circumstances, sociology apparently does not attract its share of the brightest professionally motivated students into its graduate departments. In 1961 a national cross section of 34,000 graduating seniors was surveyed to determine, among other things, the relation between choice of graduate department and academic ability, as measured by an index combining cumulative grade-point average and school selectivity. Ability scores were divided into three levels: (1) above the average for all students planning to go on to graduate or professional study, (2) below the average for future graduate students but above the average for seniors in general, and (3) below the average for graduating seniors in general. The most general conclusion was that the behavioral and social sciences tend to attract women who are brighter than the men who enter the field. With respect to sociology, women entering the field are somewhat less able than women entering other graduate fields; and men planning graduate study in sociology are not only less able than men in other behavioral and social sciences, but also below the calibre of graduating seniors in general.[8]

These facts underscore the importance of strengthening undergraduate education in sociology, to which we shall address a number of recommendations in Chapter 6.


## GRADUATE TRAINING IN SOCIOLOGY

If we regard sociology in terms of its training for advanced degrees, the same pattern of rapid growth appears as in undergraduate

---

1960, 37 percent of students enrolled in doctoral departments but not yet accepted as PhD candidates were women; the figure drops to 32 percent of master's degrees conferred, 19 percent of graduate students accepted as PhD candidates, and 14 percent of all PhD degrees conferred. Sibley, *op. cit.*, p. 51.

[8] James A. Davis, *Great Aspirations* (Chicago: Aldine Publishing Company, 1964), pp. 157–58. Similar conclusions emerge from an analysis of Graduate Record Examination Scores. See Sibley, *op. cit.*, pp. 78–83.

teaching. Figure 5-2 indicates the actual number of doctor's degrees granted in the past ten years and the anticipated number for the next ten years. Between 1957 and 1967 the number of PhD's rose from 134 to 327 and it is expected to rise to a figure of 560 by 1977. In the past

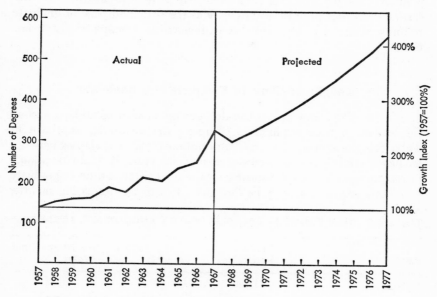

**FIGURE 5-2 SOCIOLOGY DOCTORAL DEGREES ACTUALLY AWARDED, 1957–67, AND PROJECTED TO 1977**

Source: Office of Education for 1957–67 degrees; *The Behavioral and Social Sciences: Outlook and Needs* (Englewood Cliffs, N.J.: Prentice-Hall, Inc., 1969), Appendix D, for projections 1968–77.

decade sociology has consistently produced a modest proportion of the total doctorates granted in all the behavioral and social sciences— between 8 and 9 percent.[9] The rate of growth for master's degrees is even more impressive. Some 515 master's degrees were granted in 1957, 1,193 in 1967, and the number is expected to rise to 3,300 by 1977.

[9] *Doctorate Recipients from United States Universities, 1958–1966,* NAS-NRC Publication, Publication No. 1489 (Washington, 1967). Prepared by the Office of Scientific Personnel. Table 1, pp. 7–8. (History and linguistics are included in the behavioral and social sciences.)

In the face of this demographic challenge, many departments have responded with considerable imagination and many are attempting to plan systematically for the even greater challenge of the coming decade. At the same time, there persist a number of dissatisfactions with the graduate training program in sociology in American institutions—dissatisfactions that promise to intensify as the scale and pace of graduate training continue to increase. Let us review these points of dissatisfaction:

## Length of Time to Complete the Doctorate

Sociology enjoys the dubious distinction of ranking among the leaders in time required to complete the doctorate, as shown in Table 5-4. For sociologists a median of almost ten years elapses between bachelor's and doctor's degrees—ten precious years, it might be added, of research productivity. Almost six years of registered time in graduate school are required. It may be that these figures are decreasing slightly;

**TABLE 5-4    TIME ELAPSED—BACCALAUREATE TO DOCTORATE, 1958–1966\***

| Field | Total Population | Time Elapsed (Years) | Registered Time (Years) |
|---|---|---|---|
| Sociology | 1,760 | 9.5 | 5.7 |
| History | 3,921 | 9.4 | 5.7 |
| Anthropology, archaeology | 740 | 9.4 | 5.3 |
| Geography | 574 | 9.3 | 5.3 |
| Political science, public admin., international relations | 2,628 | 9.2 | 5.1 |
| Economics, econometrics | 4,000 | 8.6 | 4.9 |

\* Source: *Doctorate Recipients from United States Universities, 1958–66*, NAS-NRC Publication No. 1489, Washington, 1967, prepared by the Office of Scientific Personnel, Tables 1, 14.

the median years from bachelor's to doctor's degree was 9.6 in 1958–60, 9.1 in 1964–66.[10] But the decrease, if it exists at all, is discouragingly slow.

Although the reasons for this relatively long delay are not fully understood, we might speculate about a number of factors that are likely to contribute to it. First, as we have seen, future sociologists normally choose their field relatively late in their educational careers. As a result they are more likely to be required, or feel the necessity, to improve their backgrounds before moving into full-time pursuit of graduate work.

Second, if the calibre of entering graduate students in sociology is somewhat lower than in other specialties, this might slow the process of completing the numerous and diverse tasks required for the doctorate.

Third, many argue that increased financial support for graduate students would facilitate more nearly full-time work in the doctoral program and thus an acceleration toward completion of the degree. To be sure, sociology is now no worse off than other behavioral and social sciences—and better off than some—both in proportion of graduate students supported and in support given (see Table 5-5). Furthermore, their share of fellowships and traineeships, which presumably permit more nearly full-time pursuit of doctoral work than assistantships normally do, compares favorably with some other behavioral and social sciences (see Table 5-6). Nevertheless, a case can be made on absolute grounds that an increase in proportion and amount of graduate-student support would facilitate completion of the doctorate. We base our case for this increase on two arguments: (1) Wider and greater support would free students from those kinds of employment that are irrelevant to the pursuit of work toward the degree. (2) A higher level of support, especially during the later stages of doctoral work, would discourage students from taking full-time teaching positions before finishing their doctoral dissertations. At the present time the level of fellowship support is perhaps only half that of a starting salary in a college or university. Furthermore, this discrepancy in income promises to increase in the future as the demand for sociologists continues to outstrip supply (see pp. 142–46).

Fourth, progress toward the doctorate is probably impeded by the

---

[10] *Ibid.*, Table 14, pp. 66–68.

TABLE 5-5 FINANCIAL AID, NEWLY ENTERING GRADUATE STUDENTS, AUTUMN 1967 *

| Financial Aid | Anthropology | Economics[a] | Geography | History | Linguistics | Political Science | Psychology[b] | Sociology[c] | Total |
|---|---|---|---|---|---|---|---|---|---|
| Percentage of those accepted into graduate school who were offered financial aid | 33 | 32 | 45 | 26 | 30 | 28 | 52 | 37 | 35 |
| Percentage of those enrolled in graduate school who received financial aid | 46 | 52 | 63 | 43 | 45 | 43 | 70 | 60 | 53 |
| Average *amount* of financial aid per entering student | $3,080 | $2,990 | $2,928 | $2,647 | $3,376 | $2,877 | $3,007 | $2,905 | $2,910 |

* Source: Departmental Questionnaire.
[a] Excluding agricultural economics.
[b] Excluding educational psychology.
[c] Excluding rural sociology.

persistence of various requirements that may be obsolete from the standpoint of developing the professional competence of scholars. Foreign-language examinations are most often singled out for attack but, in

**TABLE 5-6   TYPES OF MAJOR SUPPORT, SELECTED SOCIAL AND BEHAVIORAL SCIENCES, FALL 1966 (as percentages of full-time graduate students in PhD-granting departments) ***

| Support | Anthropology | Economics | Political Science | Psychology | Sociology |
|---|---|---|---|---|---|
| Fellowships and traineeships | 36 | 31 | 32 | 38 | 39 |
| Teaching assistantships | 15 | 19 | 14 | 19 | 19 |
| Research assistantships | 8 | 12 | 7 | 16 | 12 |
| Other support* | 41 | 38 | 47 | 27 | 30 |
| Total | 100 | 100 | 100 | 100 | 100 |

* Source: National Science Foundation, *Graduate Student Support and Manpower Resources in Graduate Science Education, Fall 1965–Fall 1966*, NSF 68–13, June 1968, p. 90.
ª Mostly self-support.

addition, academic departments and university administrations are generally conservative in changing features such as residence requirements, course requirements, the structure of qualifying examinations, and so on.

## Quality of Training

In his survey of institutions of graduate training in sociology, Sibley singled out many aspects of graduate programs that produce dissatisfaction among faculty and graduate students. Among these were superficiality of coverage in core courses in sociological theory; inadequacy of training in mathematics, statistics, and computer skills; and inadequate training in foreign languages that might be useful for research. His open-ended survey of some 400 sociology PhD's in 1960 evoked a substantial number of sentiments concerning deficiencies in their own doctoral training—especially deficiencies in research training, mathematics and statistics, training in related disciplines, and training in theory, philosophy, and logic.[11]

### Style of Training

In many graduate schools the first year is marked by under-developed systems of faculty advising and large classes—some as large as seventy-five or one hundred students in major institutions—so that the entering graduate student is not provided with an environment conducive to the development of professional commitment to the discipline. In later years the student is likely to find himself as a teaching assistant in a large course, with little opportunity for effective interaction with the senior professor, or as a research assistant performing tasks that are not relevant to his major doctoral program. Such arrangements do not encourage the consolidation of professional commitment.

Acknowledging the persistence of these deficiencies and recognizing the demands that are going to be placed on graduate departments in the coming decade, we shall present a number of recommendations for strengthening graduate training in Chapter 6.

## THE IMPENDING MANPOWER SHORTAGE
## IN SOCIOLOGY

As we have seen, the numbers of undergraduate and graduate students are going to increase even more rapidly in the coming decade than they have in the past. Will the capacity of the profession to educate and train these numbers increase as rapidly?

One way to answer this question is to compare the projections of output of doctor's degrees (supply of talent) with the projected manpower needs of the educational institutions (demand for talent). We have already presented (in Figure 5-2) the expected contour of the growth curve of production of doctorates. On the demand side, we may turn to the estimates of the anticipated growth of departments over the next ten years provided by chairmen on the departmental questionnaire ad-

[11] Sibley, *op. cit.*, Chapters 8 and 9, and p. 162.

ministered by the Behavioral and Social Science Survey. The estimated
needs for sociology faculty in PhD-granting institutions grew from a total
of an actual 1,391 full-time equivalent faculty members in autumn 1966
to an estimated 2,052 in autumn 1971 and to an estimated 2,600 in
autumn 1976—a percentage growth of 87 percent from 1966 to 1976.

How does the estimate of future demand for faculty members compare with the estimate of future supply of doctorates in sociology? An
elaborate set of computations addressed directly to this question was

FIGURE 5-3  CUMULATIVE DEFICIENCY OF SOCIOLOGY DOC-
TORATE-HOLDERS JOINING FULLTIME COLLEGE AND UNIVER-
SITY STAFFS

Source:    Courtesy of Abbott Ferriss, Russell Sage Foundation.

prepared for the Behavioral and Social Science Survey by Abbott Ferriss.[12] These computations took into account replacements for deaths
and retirements, as well as an estimate of the number of PhD's taking
employment outside the colleges and universities. Figure 5-3 shows the
results of these computations for sociology. Of course they can be

[12] See also Abbott Ferriss, "Forecasting supply and demand of sociologists," *American Sociologist*, 3 (1968), 225–234.

regarded only as rough approximations, since they are based on estimates that will have to be revised as conditions change. Nevertheless,
the results for sociology are of such a magnitude as to justify some apprehension. If present trends continue, it appears not only that sociology
is going to face a difficult market situation in the next decade—with
supply lagging far behind demand—but also that its cumulative deficiency of full-time doctorates is among the most severe in the behavioral
and social sciences. It is also apparent that an enormous effort must be
made to expand and accelerate the output of PhD's if the anticipated
rate of growth of educational institutions is to be possible.

We must add one more complication to this prospect of a critical
shortage of manpower in the coming years—a complication arising from
the fact that educational institutions now regarded as less prestigious are

**TABLE 5-7   ACTUAL AND EXPECTED PhD PRODUCTION BY CARTTER CATE-
GORY (data corrected for item non-response and departmental non-response)**

| Cartter Ranking | Total PhD-Granting Sociology Departments | 1967 (Actual) | | 1972 (Estimate) | | 1977 (Estimate) | |
|---|---|---|---|---|---|---|---|
| | | Total PhD's | Index | Total PhD's | Index | Total PhD's | Index |
| Dist./Strong | 17 | 175 | 100 | 250 | 143 | 300 | 171 |
| Good/Adequate | 17 | 76 | 100 | 170 | 224 | 240 | 316 |
| Not ranked | 29 | 96 | 100 | 230 | 240 | 350 | 365 |
| Not included | 16 | 16 | 100 | 100 | 625 | 170 | 1,063 |
| Total | 79 | 363 | 100 | 740ᵃ | 204 | 1060 | 292 |

Source: Departmental Questionnaire. Cartter categories based on those established in *An Assessment of Quality in Graduate Education* by Allan M. Cartter,
American Council on Education, Washington, D.C., 1966.

ᵃ Detail may not add to total because of rounding.

expected to increase their production of doctorates at a much faster rate
than are the more prestigious ones. To calculate the effect of this expected differential growth, the departments of the universities surveyed
were divided into four categories—those ranked "distinguished or

strong" in the Cartter survey of graduate education;[18] those ranked "good or adequate"; those not ranked at all; and those now granting PhD's, but not included in the Cartter survey. Then the departmental estimates of future growth were totaled for each category. The results are shown in Table 5-7. According to these admittedly approximate estimates, the

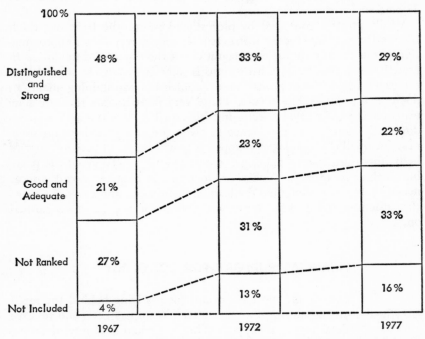

**FIGURE 5-4   EXPECTED PERCENTAGES OF PhD'S PRODUCED BY INSTITUTIONS WITHIN EACH CARTTER CATEGORY**

Source:   Table 5-7 before rounding.

most prestigious sociology departments will not quite double their PhD output by 1977, while the least prestigious ones will produce nearly a four-fold increase; the intermediate categories will approximately triple

[18] Allan M. Cartter, *An Assessment of Quality in Graduate Education* (Washington: American Council on Education, 1966).

their outputs. Figure 5-4 translates these trends into expected percentages of PhD's produced by institutions within each category as presently ranked. If departmental ambitions are realized, the most prestigious departments will drop from producing 48 percent of the PhD's at present to producing 29 percent of them in 1977; those that were not ranked in the Cartter survey will increase their production from 27 percent to 33 percent.

While prestige conferred by professional peers—the basis on which the Cartter rankings were constructed—is only a very rough approximation of quality of training, the magnitude of the expected differentials in growth among the various institutions is sufficiently large to suggest that the expected pattern of growth poses problems of maintaining quality in doctoral training in the future. Those very departments that are now experiencing difficulty in recruiting high-quality faculty—and will undoubtedly continue to experience it, given the anticipated competitiveness for qualified sociologists—apparently will begin to play an increasingly important role in training doctoral candidates. To avoid the possible decline in average quality of doctoral training, it would appear necessary both to strengthen the leading institutions and to work toward strengthening the present training programs of the less-distinguished ones.

## FINANCIAL SUPPORT FOR SOCIOLOGY

One of the most important factors lying behind the rapid growth of sociology during the past fifteen years has been the massive growth of federal financial support. This has taken a variety of forms, including research grants, training grants, fellowships, and loans. Let us first survey the scope and distribution of research support—the largest item of federal support—and then raise a few questions about some possible implications of the growth of federal support for the profession.

### Federal Research Support

Figure 5-5 shows the actual and estimated growth of federal obligations for research in sociology between 1959 and 1969. In the 1950's the Department of Defense, primarily the Air Force and the

Navy, began to extend substantial support to sociological research. Not long thereafter the health-related agencies (National Institutes of Health and National Institute of Mental Health) began to sponsor sociological research. The explosive rate of growth occurred in the middle 1960's, as more agencies began to include sociological research in their budgets. By

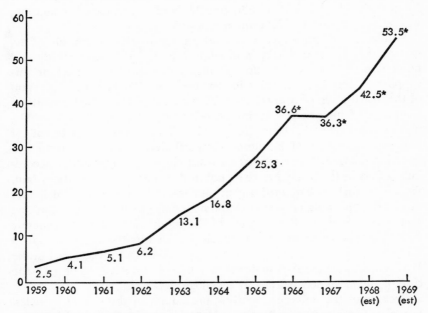

**FIGURE 5-5    FEDERAL OBLIGATIONS FOR RESEARCH IN SOCI-OLOGY (millions of dollars)**

Source:    National Science Foundation, *Federal Funds for Research,* etc., Volumes IX–XVII, 1959–67.
*Figures for 1966, 1967, 1968 (est.), and 1969 (est.) have been adjusted for reporting errors (see footnote 14 for 1967 adjustment; similar adjustments have been made for the other three years).

1967 the Department of Health, Education, and Welfare alone contributed $17.7 million to sociological research, with the National Institute of Mental Health ($15.8 million) assuming the largest share of the Health, Education, and Welfare budget. In the same year the Office of Economic Opportunity contributed $10.1 million, the National Science

Foundation $3.2 million, and the Department of Defense $2.0 million.

Most research supported by the government falls in the "applied" category. About two thirds of the support provided by the National Institute of Mental Health and three quarters of the support provided by the Office of Economic Opportunity was listed as "applied" in 1967. The major sources of "basic research" were the National Institute of Mental Health with $5.1 million and the National Science Foundation, whose total support of $3.2 million was so listed.[14]

While these figures give a general picture of the magnitude of research support for sociology, and while Figure 5-5 shows a steady and rapid rate of growth, they do not reveal the selective impact of this support on the different fields in the discipline. To gain an impression of the distribution of research support, we went to the annual reports of a number of important granting agencies for fiscal year 1967—the Department of Health, Education, and Welfare, the Department of Defense, the Office of Economic Opportunity, and the National Science Foundation. We classified all research grants in sociology according to field in the discipline (e.g., political sociology, stratification, family, and so on). We defined a grant as "research in sociology" if it met one of the following criteria: (a) the materials provided by the granting agency indicated that the recipient of the grant belonged to an academic department of sociology; (b) materials provided by the agency classified the project as sociological; (c) the principal investigator was listed in the 1967 Directory of the American Sociological Association, or (d) the title of the grant seemed clearly sociological.

Because of the different reporting procedures of the several agencies, our classification is admittedly only an approximate one. Moreover, assigning a research grant to a field is difficult, because our own listing of fields is necessarily arbitrary and because most sociological research

[14] Figures are taken from Tables C–26, C–45 and C–64, in "Federal Obligations in Psychological and Social Sciences by Agency and Discipline, Fiscal Year 1967," in *Federal Funds for Research, Development, and Other Scientific Activities,* FY 1967, 1968 and 1969, NSF 68–27, Vol. XVII. The amount of sociological research supported by the Office of Education is not discernible from these figures, since the classificatory categories are "psychology" and "other social science." *Note:* We have reduced the published total for sociology for the Department of Health, Education and Welfare from $31.3 million to $17.7 million to account for an error which assigned $13.7 million of the Social and Rehabilitation Service's obligations to sociology.

deals simultaneously with several different topics. For example, research comparing the job aspirations of Negro and white high school students could be classified under "social psychology," "sociology of work," "race relations," and "educational sociology." We attempted to discern the primary focus of research topics, and assign them to appropriate single fields. Because of these methodological problems, our calculations should be regarded only as rough approximations of the true picture of the distribution of research support by the granting agencies.

Despite these difficulties, a number of general inferences can be drawn from the distribution of support shown in Table 5-8. A number of fields in "applied" areas are among the most heavily supported—notably deviance (including crime and delinquency), race, health and medicine, and some aspects of socialization. This suggests that even for relatively "basic" research, support tends to be greatest in fields that are concerned with society's major social problems. Two fields—political sociology and organizations and institutions—not only were liberally supported, but also were supported by a large number of agencies. By contrast, small-group research received almost all its support from one agency, the National Science Foundation. And finally, some fields were neglected almost altogether. In particular, the results of Table 5-8 confirm our speculations in Chapter 2 that collective behavior and the sociology of religion are significantly underfinanced by federal agencies. (It may be, however, that some research on collective behavior was supported under other headings, such as "deviance" or "race.") Although many of the projects may have had theoretical aspects, we found virtually no awards that could be judged to support theoretical analysis as such.

From the available materials it is difficult to ascertain the causes of the particular distribution of research support in Table 5-8. In some cases the policies of the granting agencies may lay great emphasis on some fields and little emphasis on others. In other cases there may have been either an abundance or a shortage of research applications of high quality. And in still other cases an agency may gain a certain reputation among potential researchers, whether deserved or not, and this may influence the flow of applications to that agency. A full understanding of the causes awaits a better basis for classifying research projects, a systematic comparison of the distribution of applications with the distribution of awards, and an analysis of trends of support over time.

**TABLE 5-8  SUPPORT FOR SOCIOLOGY  FISCAL YEAR 1967 (number of grants by subfield and agency, expenditure by field)**

| Sociology Subfield | Department of Defense | Health, Education, and Welfare | National Science Foundation | Office of Economic Opportunity | Total Grants | Total Funds (000's) |
|---|---|---|---|---|---|---|
| Health and medicine | – | 31 | 1 | 1 | 33 | $2,666 |
| Political | 12 | 6 | 10 | 2 | 30 | 2,020 |
| Stratification | – | 6 | 3 | 4 | 13 | 1,730 |
| Deviance | – | 21 | 5 | 2 | 28 | 1,458 |
| Socialization | – | 23 | 8 | – | 31 | 1,208 |
| Race | – | 25[a] | 2 | – | 27 | 1,169 |
| Organizations and institutions | 8 | 8 | 9 | 2 | 27 | 1,169 |
| Small groups | 1 | 2 | 22 | – | 25 | 860 |
| Work | 3 | 12 | 5 | 2 | 22 | 859 |
| Methodology | 1 | 7 | 9 | – | 17 | 803 |
| Social change | 7 | 4 | 1 | 1 | 13 | 741 |
| Social psychology | – | 4 | 7 | – | 11 | 590 |
| Family | – | 9 | 1 | – | 10 | 326 |
| Urban | – | 8 | 3 | – | 11 | 324 |
| Law | – | 1 | 2 | 2 | 5 | 207 |
| Comparative studies | 1 | 1 | 1 | – | 3 | 82 |
| Education | – | 4 | – | – | 4 | 77 |
| Population | 1 | 3 | 2 | – | 6 | 65 |
| Religion | – | – | 1 | – | 1 | 28 |
| Systematic theory | – | – | 2 | – | 2 | 28 |
| Collective behavior | – | – | 1 | – | 1 | 27 |
| Culture | – | – | – | – | – | – |
| Other | 1 | 7 | 1 | – | 9 | 143 |
| Total | 35 | 182 | 96 | 16 | 236 | $16,570 |

Sources: Reports of listed agencies for fiscal year 1967. Reports varied from letters written in response to our request, xeroxed typed tables, and printed annual reports of research supported.

[a] Four of the projects classified under "Race" could have been classified with equal justification under "Urban."

### Support and the Profession

What is the general allocation of financial resources within the profession, and what are the general origins of these resources?

In the questionnaire survey of universities conducted by the Behavioral and Social Science Survey Committee, PhD-granting departments were asked to provide an account of the expenditure for various categories (academic personnel, research personnel, secretarial services, permanent equipment, etc.) in fiscal year 1967. To see how these are allocated both within sociology departments and relative to anthropology, economics, and psychology, we totaled the expenditures both by category and field, and entered these totals as percentages of all such expenditures for the behavioral and social sciences. In addition, we calculated the percentage of full-time equivalent faculty for each field in relation to the total. Table 5-9 shows the results of these computations.

Interestingly, there is a notably small difference between percentage of total expenditure and percentage of total faculty, except in psychology. Sociology faculties constitute .115 of the faculty of all the behavioral and social sciences, and they spend .115 of the total financial resources for all fields. The same holds for the totals in anthropology and economics. Psychology, however, reveals a significant discrepancy, with percentage of total expenditures considerably higher than percentage of faculty. This apparently is traceable to the exceptional expenditure for permanent equipment, especially laboratory facilities in psychology.

When Table 5-9 is read closely, sociology appears to spend relatively less on research personnel (except for support personnel) and relatively less on permanent equipment. It is difficult to predict future changes in these proportions, but if the trend toward large-scale, quantitative research in sociology continues as rapidly in the next quarter-century as it has in the one just passed, the needs for increased expenditure on research personnel and permanent equipment (particularly computational equipment) will call for more rapid growth of expenditures in these categories than in the others. If the trend toward experimental small-group research in sociology also accelerates, this is likely to call for a relatively rapid increase in expenditures for permanent equipment (particularly laboratory equipment).

TABLE 5-9 EXPENDITURES OF SELECTED DEPARTMENTS AS PERCENTAGES OF TOTALS FOR ALL BEHAVIORAL AND SOCIAL SCIENCE DEPARTMENTS

| Expenditure Item | % for Sociology | Rank for Sociology | % for Anthropology | Rank for Anthropology | % for Economics[a] | Rank for Economics | % for Psychology[b] | Rank for Psychology |
|---|---|---|---|---|---|---|---|---|
| Fringe benefits | .137 | 1 | .066 | 3 | .199 | 2 | .271 | 7 |
| Secretarial services | .131 | 2 | .054 | 6 | .156 | 6 | .313 | 6 |
| Research support personnel | .130 | 3 | .076 | 1 | .127 | 8 | .468 | 2 |
| Teaching assistants | .124 | 4 | .043 | 8 | .183 | 3 | .249 | 8 |
| Academic staff (instructor and above) | .116 | 5 | .055 | 5 | .165 | 5 | .224 | 9 |
| Other (supplies, phone, etc.) | .105 | 6 | .075 | 2 | .141 | 7 | .401 | 3 |
| Research professors and associates | .099 | 7 | .051 | 7 | .205 | 1 | .336 | 5 |
| Research assistants | .097 | 8 | .034 | 9 | .166 | 4 | .378 | 4 |
| Permanent equipment | .065 | 9 | .060 | 4 | .054 | 9 | .706 | 1 |
| Total of items in table | .115 | | .055 | | .164 | | .272 | |
| Full-time faculty, FTE[c] | .115 | | .055 | | .162 | | .215 | |

Source: Departmental Questionnaire.
[a] Excluding agricultural economics.
[b] Excluding educational psychology.
[c] Full-time Equivalents.

What are the general sources of financial support for sociology departments? On the departmental questionnaires the data were classified into "General University Sources," referring mainly to state and endowment income and tuition fees, and "Other Sources," referring to support from government, foundations, and private donors. The federal government contributes most to the latter category.

**TABLE 5-10   PERCENTAGE OF FUNDS FROM GRANTS AND CONTRACTS BY EXPENDITURE CATEGORY FOR SOCIOLOGY AND OTHER BEHAVIORAL AND SOCIAL SCIENCE DISCIPLINES**

| Category | Sociology | All Other Fields | Total |
|---|---|---|---|
| Research support personnel | 86 | 69 | 71 |
| Research assistants | 69 | 67 | 67 |
| Research professors and associates | 65 | 65 | 65 |
| Permanent equipment | 31 | 62 | 60 |
| Other (supplies, phone, etc.) | 53 | 52 | 52 |
| Secretarial services | 28 | 28 | 28 |
| Fringe benefits | 25 | 20 | 20 |
| Academic staff (instructor and above) | 14 | 10 | 11 |
| Teaching assistants | 6 | 4 | 4 |
| Total | 23 | 21 | 21 |

Source: Departmental Questionnaire.

Table 5-10 summarizes the percentages of funds from these two sources for the various categories of expenditure in sociology and compares them with the total for the other behavioral and social sciences. The bottom row indicates that about a fifth (21 percent) of all fields' expenditures comes from sources outside the university, and that sociology's percentage (23 percent) is slightly higher than the whole.

Viewing the particular categories, we observe that the percentage for sociology is higher than those for the other disciplines in all categories except permanent equipment (which is dominated by psychology) and secretarial services. Some of these differences are quite small but the differences for academic staff (14 percent for sociology to 10 percent for all the rest) and teaching assistants (6 percent for sociology to 4 percent for all the rest) become more significant when it is remembered that these categories make up about 70 percent of departmental budgets in sociology as well as in the other behavioral and social science disciplines.

From one standpoint, sociologists might look with pleasure on the fact that their field is not disadvantaged—and perhaps is slightly favored—relative to federal and other outside sources of support, since this support makes possible both positions and facilities necessary for the pursuit of important professional activities. It should also be noted, however, that such support may make for some precariousness and instability, especially if it is used in any substantial way to finance teaching and other internal university activities. Federal support is likely to fluctuate from year to year—given the swings in politics and international relations—and these budgetary fluctuations are very unsettling, particularly if substantial percentages of university budgets are tied to external sources. Furthermore, federal support is often earmarked. As we have indicated, external funding for research in sociology tends to be concentrated in areas that currently excite the greatest public concern. Desirable as such expenditures may be socially or politically, they are likely to force universities continuously to shift the research and teaching activities of too great a proportion of their personnel, thus threatening the balance of research and teaching essential for the cumulative growth of scientific disciplines.

## CONCLUDING REMARKS

One major conclusion that emerges from our survey is that sociology now enjoys both the blessings and the curses of explosive growth on many fronts at once. It has produced much significant research in many of its fields, as well as many promising theoretical formulations; but it has not been able to consolidate these ingredients into sufficient theories of social behavior. It has rapidly expanded its teaching and training functions, but is experiencing a number of threats to continuing quality in the face of the onslaught of numbers. It has grown enormously in relevance to the social and political problems of the age, but it finds the demands for its application in excess of its capacities to provide definitive solutions. The discipline has made efforts to keep pace with increased demands, but its resources have been limited. It has benefited greatly from the generosity of external agencies, especially the federal government, but the pattern of this support has not been without complicating consequences.

The objectives of the recommendations we offer next are to foster the continued scientific and institutional growth of the discipline and to look toward the amelioration of the problems created by that very growth.

# 6

# RECOMMENDATIONS

We now present a number of recommendations to the profession, to the universities, and to the funding agencies. They are based on the facts of this report and represent the panel's best judgment concerning priorities for sociology.

## STRENGTHENING UNDERGRADUATE EDUCATION

Since the rise of academic sociology, hundreds of teachers have sparked the imagination of undergraduates, increased their understanding of social institutions, and interested them in entering the profession. Despite their achievements, we are convinced that undergraduate teaching now needs both reappraisal and improvement. We base this conviction on three sets of facts: First, the number of undergraduates now taking sociology courses has grown enormously, and this growth promises to continue, thus aggravating the familiar problems of large lecture classes and superficiality of contact between teachers and students. Second, courses in sociology tend to be offered in a uniform way to all undergraduates, even though the goals and intentions of the students are highly diversified. Third, undergraduate teaching has become a victim of the "squeeze" between the demands of professional training in the graduate schools and the rapid introduction and spread of sociology in the secondary schools. On one hand, sociology faculties

have been under steady and increasing pressure to devote time and resources to research and graduate training. Some have found these activities more rewarding than undergraduate teaching. On the other hand,
the fact that each year more and more students are exposed to sociology
in high schools means that the undergraduate curriculum, especially the
introductory course, now serves an audience that is more sophisticated
in sociology than ever before. Moreover, if the program of Sociological
Resources for Social Studies lives up to its promise, undergraduate
teachers will have even less need to "introduce" their students to
sociology.

> (1) *The Panel recommends that sociology departments
> diversify their curricula into "streams" of instruction to
> correspond better with the interests and career intentions
> of their undergraduate students.*

As an example, sociology majors might be provided with a year or
two of core sociological offerings, then be permitted to branch into
groups, such as (a) groups with serious interest in the scientific theory
and methods of sociology, and perhaps with an intention to continue
work in sociology in graduate school; (b) groups intending to enter
fields in which sociology is of general background value, for example,
primary and secondary school teaching, social work and law; (c) groups
interested in applications of sociology to public policy and social problems; and (d) groups interested in the significance of sociology as a
part of the humanistic and scientific traditions of Western thought.
Smaller schools with curricula in sociology that are not extensive enough
to permit such diversification might attain the same objective by entering into collaborative interdisciplinary and "joint-major" programs
with other departments.

We believe that these curricular innovations will equip sociology to
discharge its several obligations to undergraduate students more effectively. It will also provide sociology with more effective means of identifying, recruiting, and preparing its own future graduate students and
professionals. We do not recommend "second-class" curricula for students who do not intend to become professional sociologists. We believe,
however, that undergraduate sociology can be made both more stimu-

lating and more demanding if it is geared to its students' interests and intentions.

While college and university faculties must take the initiative in making changes in curricula, funding agencies could be prepared to supply funds for launching, implementing, and evaluating new curricula and teaching methods. Specifically, funding agencies could supply funds for equipment, facilities, and ancillary personnel necessary to implement such innovations.

(2) *The Panel recommends that empirical research be a part of undergraduate teaching from the start.*

Undergraduates should collect, analyze, and interpret sociological data, as well as read or hear about others' interpretations. We recommend first-hand research, including involvement in interview surveys, participant observation, secondary analysis, and research into archives, as a device to bring the field alive for the student by involving him directly in sociological investigations. In addition, these exercises in research will lay the groundwork for acquiring skills necessary for research by those who intend to become professional sociologists.

As a corollary, we recommend that shared-time computers be given high priority in departmental planning, because they are a powerful means for teaching advanced quantitative approaches to undergraduates. Preliminary experiments at Dartmouth and other colleges have found that practical experience with computers provides an excellent basis for acquiring essential skills and knowledge in sociology. In recommending the expanded use of computers, however, we caution that these opportunities must not be permitted to overshadow training in other types of research—informal observation, analysis of historical documents, logic of theory construction, for example—that are also essential to many lines of learning in sociology.

Once again, the responsibility for initiating programs that involve students in empirical research and quantitative analysis lies with the colleges and universities. Funding agencies could be prepared, however, to supply funds for laboratory facilities, computer space and equipment, specialized libraries, and ancillary personnel necessary to implement programs of instruction. Support would provide not only for initiating and implementing instruction in empirical research, but also for systematically evaluating the results of such instruction.

(3) *The Panel recommends that the American Sociological Association continue and intensify its interest in undergraduate teaching as a part of its professional activities.*

The Association's efforts might move in several directions. First, building on the work of Sociological Resources for Social Studies, the Association should plan and seek large-scale funding for improving undergraduate curricula, especially introductory offerings. The Association has begun explorations of these possibilities, and we urge that they continue these. Second, a significant portion of the annual national and regional meetings might be set aside for demonstration and discussion of teaching innovations in secondary schools and colleges. The Association might seek funds to sponsor special conferences and workshops on undergraduate teaching. Third, the Association might expand efforts such as the Visiting Scientist Program, sponsored by the National Science Foundation, which brings scholars from the larger institutions with graduate training and research programs to smaller colleges. Finally, the Association should continue to raise the priority of dissemination, discussion, and evaluation of information about instructional programs. We welcome *The American Sociologist*'s recent intensification of interest in pedagogical matters, and we hope it will continue this, even if it requires expansion of the size of the journal. Attention might also be given to developing a vehicle—perhaps a journal—that would provide secondary school instructors with materials and teaching suggestions for sociology courses.

## STRENGTHENING GRADUATE EDUCATION

The excellence of an academic discipline depends upon the insights and capacities of those who create and sustain it. For this reason alone, its training functions must be given the highest priority. As we observed in Chapter 5, sociology, like the other behavioral and social sciences, has been asked to expand its training operations greatly in the past ten years and will be asked to do so in the next ten.

We also discovered, however, that for a variety of reasons graduate training in sociology is not especially efficient and leaves much to be desired in its content and style. We believe that our recommendations to strengthen undergraduate education are relevant to graduate training as well; if implemented, they would have the effect of upgrading the quality of students applying to graduate schools in sociology. In addition, however, we present a number of recommendations for the organization and support of graduate training itself.

We turn first to maintenance of standards for admission to graduate schools. As we have seen, the market for trained sociologists will probably be very tight in the next decade. We are apprehensive that the resultant pressure to produce PhD's in great numbers may lead simply to headlong expansion, and that this expansion may pose a threat to quality in graduate admissions. Furthermore, because the rate of expansion of graduate training will be higher in those institutions now regarded as relatively less distinguished, the importance of maintaining high standards is all the more important.

> (4) *The Panel recommends that universities and departments strive to maintain high standards for graduate admissions where they are high, and raise standards where they are low.*

Unfortunately, such a recommendation reads like one of those ringing endorsements of virtue that typically leads neither to implementation nor to results. We venture it, however, because we anticipate special problems in maintaining quality for sociology—problems associated with its anticipated rate of growth—and we wish to bring these problems to the attention of departments and graduate schools.

A second major responsibility for departments is to continue their efforts to improve the quality of training for graduate students. As we indicated in Chapter 5, a number of facets of graduate training should be strengthened: methodological, statistical, and core-theory training; training in mathematics and the use of computers; training in interdisciplinary work with the other social sciences, and training in the application of sociology in other fields—in law, medicine, education, and public policy, for example. In addition to these apparent and widely recognized deficits in sociological training, however, we point to one further deficit: inadequate training of teachers.

At the present time, too many graduate students receive their "teacher training"—if, indeed, it deserves that term—as unsupervised "teaching assistants" in large undergraduate courses. Too often the role of teaching assistant commands only low status. And finally, the role of teaching assistant is too often confused. The teaching assistant is frequently regarded (and often regards himself) as one third teacher, one third student, and one third hired hand. The situation of the teaching assistant, in short, is conducive neither to very effective training nor to very high morale.

> (5) *The Panel recommends that universities and departments provide for the training of college-level teachers of sociology as an integral part of their regular graduate training programs.*

Our recommendation calls for emphasizing the role of "teaching apprentice," which would constitute a more integral part of graduate training. The typical graduate student might be expected to teach for a year or more under supervision, assuming more independence and responsibility as training proceeds. Faculty members might give special seminars in pedagogy to teaching apprentices, either independently of or simultaneously with courses they are teaching collectively. In cases of graduate students who are fully supported from other sources, graduate departments might consider abolishing the "teaching assistantship" as a form of paid employment, and require training in instruction as one of the regular components of a graduate career, much as courses, seminars, and various types of research training are now required.

We believe that investment in programs of teaching apprenticeship will yield a variety of returns. They will improve the quality of undergraduate teaching, in which graduate students are necessarily heavily involved. They will provide conditions for firmer professional identification and commitment among graduate students, and for improving their quality as future teachers. And they will involve faculty members more in the professional training of their graduate students.

While the primary responsibility for establishing and maintaining programs in teacher training lies with academic faculties and graduate deans, governmental agencies and private foundations could entertain applications for funds required to experiment with and initiate these programs.

> (6) *The Panel recommends that governmental and foundation programs of financial support for graduate students be expanded.*

As we have observed, two of the most important, but not the only, factors that create the long lapse of time between the bachelor's and doctor's degrees are the necessity to take employment unrelated to graduate studies and the pressure to take full-time teaching positions before the doctoral dissertation is completed. Existing programs of support by federal agencies and private foundations could be expanded in three ways: (a) provision of "career support" for a larger proportion of graduate students to complete their degrees within a given number of years; (b) provision of "dissertation awards" of one or two years' duration for employed teachers of sociology who have completed all doctoral requirements except their dissertations; (c) extension of the practice of providing direct research costs of dissertations as well as tuition and living costs for recipients. (See Chapter 9 of the report, *The Behavioral and Social Sciences: Outlook and Needs*).

In recommending these programs of increased support we assume that recipients would be required not to seek supplementary employment during the period covered by the support and that departments would establish practicable time limitations for the completion of the several requirements for the doctorate.

> (7) *The Panel recommends that the federal government expand its support of research-training programs in departments and organized research units.*

As a supplement to individual fellowship and project research support, government agencies have provided funds for research-training programs. Sociology has benefited particularly from the funding supplied by the National Institute of Mental Health and the National

Science Foundation. In recommending expansion of this type of support, we suggest the following guidelines to policy:

(a) In grants to organized research units, high priority should be given to projects that include training of graduate students.

(b) Some departmental training grants should focus on specific aspects of sociology—demography, small-group investigations, medical sociology, or mathematical techniques, for example.

(c) Other departmental grants, however, should support general sociological training without reference to specific subject-matter or research methods. The primary criteria for these grants should be the quality of the training program proposed by the department, and the general quality of its faculty. We see this general support as a kind of balance to the support of specific subject-matter programs. A balance is necessary to encourage the growth and consolidation of a solid base of theory and research, and to avoid either famine or force-feeding of any of the discipline's fields.

> (8) *The Panel recommends that the American Sociological Association continue and intensify its interest in the recruitment and training of graduate students in its professional activities.*

The Association might expand efforts such as conferences on ways to improve graduate training in sociology, similar to the series sponsored by the National Institute of Mental Health; devoting a larger portion of the annual and regional meetings for discussion of standards of admission, different types of training programs, and the training of teachers of sociology in graduate school; and increasing the amount of space in *The American Sociologist* devoted to problems of graduate training.

## STRENGTHENING SOCIOLOGICAL KNOWLEDGE

In Chapter 2 we surveyed the development of perhaps a dozen sub-fields in sociology. We were able to identify several ingredients that are essential for accumulation of reliable scientific knowledge. Among these ingredients are an adequate base of empirical data, an adequate theoretical framework for interpreting data, adequate means for disseminating and discussing new knowledge, and adequate time and financial support for research. We observed, however, that present institutional arrangements—academic departments and research units—do not always provide the optimum conditions for the pursuit of ambitious cooperative research. And we argued that patterns of crash support for sensitive areas of policy or social problems are probably not conducive to the development of an integrated balance of the ingredients necessary for scientific advance. In the light of these several arguments, we present a number of recommendations for institutional arrangements and types of support that we believe will facilitate the growth of scientific knowledge in sociology.

> (9) *The Panel recommends that the federal government plan and provide support for a diversity of international, national, and regional research centers for collecting, analyzing, and disseminating various kinds of social data.*

We venture this recommendation not as a call for the immediate establishment of more research units, but rather as a general guide to long-run policy. We see no particular merit in establishing research centers as such. Possible centers should be established only after identifying substantive areas that are important either to social science or to society, studying past research efforts in those areas, estimating costs, and examining the probable implications of creating centers to undertake further work in those areas.

As a preliminary to legislation and funding, the American Sociological Association, in collaboration with other professional associations in the behavioral and social sciences and with other bodies such as the Social Science Research Council or the National Research Council, should create a planning body to prepare guidelines to be made available to the federal government and other funding sources for the development of international, national, and regional research centers for collecting, analyzing, and disseminating various kinds of social data.

Without wishing to limit the scope of future planning and funding activities, we suggest that policy be guided by four principles of diversity, listed here in terms of sociological knowledge, but of equal concern to other disciplines:

(a) Diversity of program content. Some research centers should focus on broad substantive areas of continuing sociological concern (for example, the study of formal organizations, the comparative study of religion), whereas others should focus on problem areas of more immediate social concern (for example, violence, suicide, poverty).

(b) Diversity of research methods. Some centers should be designed to develop comparative international data and archives; others to accumulate survey data on individuals, organizations, communities, and nations; others to collect first-hand data on episodes of collective behavior, community crises, action programs, and other natural events as they unfold; others to accumulate longitudinal and panel data; and still others to record the results of research based on participant observation and other informal methods. The development of sociological knowledge relies on a variety of types of data, collected in a variety of ways. This fact should underlie the establishment of research centers.

(c) Diversity of institutional arrangements. Some centers should develop in the process of strengthening existing research units; others should be newly created. Some should be affiliated with university campuses; others with regional consortia of universities; others established independently of universities; and still others established as cooperative enterprises between universities and other agencies in a number of countries. Such diversity should encourage the institutional flexibility necessary for meeting the complex requirements of social research.

(d) Diversity of disciplinary emphasis. We do not envision the proposed research centers as composed entirely of sociologists. Wherever possible, teams including members of many disciplines should be developed.

(10) *The Panel recommends that funding agencies extend their efforts to support surveys of the American population.*

Our objective in this recommendation is to extend and improve the data that are now provided by the decennial United States Census, the Current Population Survey, and by those who conduct opinion polls and other surveys of various sorts. Many of these data are valuable, but some are quite specialized, and some are collected too infrequently or irregularly to permit the construction of adequate time series. Many types of data important both to social scientists and to public agencies are gathered only inadequately by present means—data relating to migratory flows by occupation, social mobility, use of leisure time, and intergroup relations among large-city residents, to select a few examples.

We do not recommend any special format for the extended survey activity. Perhaps it should involve an extension of the operations of the Current Population Survey; perhaps it should involve the creation of a new agency; perhaps it should involve increased use of existing private and university centers for survey research; perhaps a combination of these formats would be optimal. Whatever the format, however, we suggest that survey efforts should include both (a) relatively "permanent" sets of items, repeated each year so that time trends over long periods could be constructed—trends tracing, for example, attitudes toward different minority groups, or attitudes toward family planning, and (b) surveys of particular themes, so that some depth might be attained on given topics. We also suggest that standing committees of highly qualified behavioral and social scientists be involved in the design and execution of national surveys. And finally, we suggest that these extended survey activities be coordinated with any efforts to establish a series of social indicators and to develop an annual social report (see Chapter 6 of the overall report, *The Behavioral and Social Sciences: Outlook and Needs*).

It is essential that data produced both by the proposed research centers and by extended survey activities be made publicly available on a regular basis. For example, survey data might be made available in the form of data cards or tapes for universities, colleges, and research centers for further analysis and publication. In addition to extending the data base now generated by the United States Census and other survey activities, this practice would have the advantage of encouraging more replication and more continuity in research, since many investigators would work on the same data. We stress, however, that both in gathering and in making public survey and other data, adequate mechanisms must be established to safeguard respondents' privacy, anonymity, freedom of consent, and other rights (see Chapters 7 and 8 of the overall report, *The Behavioral and Social Sciences: Outlook and Needs*).

> *(11) The Panel recommends that the federal government increase financial support for basic social-scientific research in addition to its support for research designed for short-run programmatic applications.*

As we have indicated, sociological knowledge and research are clearly relevant to a great number of problems of national concern, including those fitting into the programmatic interests of governmental action agencies (education, poverty, health, crime, and so on). Because so many of these problems are immediate and pressing, sociology is often pressed—and given financial support—to produce quick findings and solutions. The resulting vicissitudes of research support are likely both to threaten the balanced scientific growth of the field and to jeopardize the accumulation of basic research.

We do not recommend that agencies with programmatic interests cease to support research, nor that sociologists cease to take an active interest in applying their research findings as conscientiously as they can to those interests. But we do recommend that a substantial portion of support for sociological research be provided mainly with concern for the excellence and feasibility of the proposed research and without special regard to immediate policy relevance. This implies continued funding of proposals initiated by one or more investigators, and evaluated by panels of disciplinary colleagues. It also implies that in some cases funding should be provided over long periods of time, to guarantee the continuity of research requiring many years to execute (for example, longitudinal studies).

We do not envision any single mechanism for providing substantial and continuous support for basic research. Perhaps the proper mechanism is to expand the behavioral and social science activities of the National Science Foundation; perhaps it is to create a new National Social Science Foundation; perhaps programmatic agencies should devote increasing proportions of their funds to basic research; perhaps some combination of different mechanisms would be optimal. Whatever the mechanisms, we wish to stress the importance of generous,

**168**                                                                        **SOCIOLOGY**

generalized support that will facilitate the growth of sociological theory
and research and secure its insulation from short-term pressures (see
Chapter 14 of the overall report, *The Behavioral and Social Sciences:
Outlook and Needs*).

> (12) *The Panel recommends that graduate schools and
> research centers establish educational programs in sociology
> for a variety of audiences.*

The major emphases of these programs would be to disseminate
sociological knowledge and to teach sociological theory and research to
important segments of the public. Examples of such programs would
be demographic methods, study of race relations, mathematical models
in sociology, comparative study of the family. Programs could vary
in length from a few weeks or a summer up to an entire year. They
could be directed toward a variety of audiences—for example, teachers of sociology who desire updated training and education, civil
servants from action agencies, and journalists and others who are responsible for interpreting sociology to the lay public through the mass media.

While graduate schools and research institutes should bear the responsibility for initiating and maintaining these programs, federal and private
agencies could provide financial support, especially in the early stages
of their development.

> (13) *The Panel recommends the publication of an annual
> review of sociology.*

The objective of this publication would be to review findings and
trends from the various fields of sociology on an annual basis. Other
disciplines have published such reviews for some time, and we believe
an annual review for sociology is overdue. The American Sociological
Association might well take the initiative in pressing for the establishment of such a review.

## SOCIOLOGY AND THE FEDERAL GOVERNMENT

We have already presented several recommendations calling for federal support and suggesting policies that might guide this

support. In these recommendations we were attempting to outline the contours of one major relationship between government and the profession—the relationship of financial sponsorship. A second major relationship arises when sociologists are asked to provide findings, advice, or solutions that may be brought to bear on the formation of social policies and the solution of social problems.

We anticipate that in the long run both federal support of research and training and the demands on sociologists to help solve pressing social problems will increase substantially. In the light of these probable changes, we suggest several arrangements that may create a relationship between the government and the profession that will be as effective as possible.

> *(14) The Panel recommends that agencies of the federal government plan for and establish standing panels to consult and advise on major social problems.*

As matters now stand, social and behavioral scientists are too often asked for consultation and advice on a "one-shot" or irregular basis. Government agencies and commissions too often "start from scratch" in seeking consultants after some crisis or disaster has struck. We recommend that agencies of the federal government consider establishing appropriate standing advisory panels, each focusing on a persistent problem area—for example, the condition of the family, the problems of the aged, youth, poverty, violence and conflict, or criminal behavior. These should be separate from panels that propose and evaluate research programs. The advisory panels, composed of behavioral and social scientists from several disciplines, would meet regularly, and would advise relevant agencies on matters of program and policy related to the substance of the agencies' missions.

> *(15) The Panel recommends that the American Sociological Association establish a permanent committee to assess and monitor the effects of federal legislation and federal spending on sociology.*

As we have seen, government support of sociology has grown to several dozens of millions of dollars per year in the past several years.

Many signs point toward a long-term increase. As we have also seen, federal spending, while fostering growth in many areas, is also likely to create problems of imbalance for the development of the field. We believe that some machinery is necessary to take continuous stock of the impact of this federal activity. The committee we suggest would be empowered to study and report—and perhaps commission research—concerning the impact of federal laws and regulations affecting research and teaching; the effects of federal spending on the development of the discipline, on graduate training, and on undergraduate education; and on the net balance of benefits and costs to the profession occasioned by programs of support.

> (16) *The Panel recommends that the American Sociological Association establish a committee to assess the effects on public policy and sociology arising from consultation and advice provided to government.*

Almost all behavioral and social scientists have ideas and opinions about the consequences that arise from efforts to apply sociological knowledge. These ideas and opinions are often conflicting and they are often based on simple articles of faith rather than solid empirical information. In this final recommendation we propose the establishment of some mechanism for objective inquiry into and evaluation of the consultative relations between the profession and the government. The committee we suggest would be empowered to study and report—and perhaps commission research—concerning the relative effectiveness of different mechanisms for consultation and advice, as well as the ways in which consultative relations with governmental agencies affect not only government policy but also research and training in sociology.

We welcome the recent increase in attention that the American Sociological Association has devoted to the ethical and political problems that arise in the relations between the profession and its various publics. In our final two recommendations above, we express the hope that the Association will devote some of its energies to the collection and analysis of data that may inform future policies and actions concerning its relations with the federal government.

# APPENDIX

CONTRIBUTORS OF MEMORANDA TO THE
SOCIOLOGY PANEL ON THE STATUS OF
VARIOUS FIELDS IN THE DISCIPLINE

Robert C. Angell, University of Michigan; Joseph Ben-David, Hebrew University, Jerusalem; James M. Beshers, Massachusetts Institute of Technology; Albert D. Biderman, Bureau of Social Science Research; Peter M. Blau, University of Chicago; David J. Bordua, University of Illinois, Urbana; Orville G. Brim, Jr., Russell Sage Foundation; Ernest Q. Campbell, Vanderbilt University; F. Stuart Chapin, Asheville, North Carolina; Lindsey Churchill, Russell Sage Foundation; Alexander L. Clark, University of Texas; John A. Clausen, University of California, Berkeley; James S. Coleman, Johns Hopkins University; Philip E. Converse, University of Michigan; LaMar T. Empey, University of Southern California; Morris F. Friedell, University of Michigan; Ronald Freedman, University of Michigan; Howard E. Freeman, Brandeis University; William A. Gamson, University of Michigan; Charles Y. Glock, University of California, Berkeley; Robert L. Hall, University of Illinois at Chicago Circle; Warren O. Hagstrom, University of Wisconsin, Madison; Philip Hauser, University of Chicago; Amos H. Hawley, University of North Carolina; Robert W. Hodge, University of Chicago; Paul Hollander, Harvard University; George C. Homans, Harvard University; Elihu Katz, Hebrew University, Jerusalem; Lewis M. Killian, University

**171**

of Connecticut; Leslie Kish, University of Michigan; Melvin L. Kohn,
National Institute of Mental Health; Charles Laughton, The Hogg
Foundation for Mental Health; Gerhard Lenski, University of North
Carolina; Gary T. Marx, Harvard University; David Mechanic, Univer-
sity of Wisconsin, Madison; Herbert Menzel, New York University;
Theodore M. Mills, State University of New York at Buffalo; William
Mitchell, University of Oregon; Wilbert E. Moore, Russell Sage Foun-
dation; Nicholas C. Mullins, Dartmouth College; Harold W. Pfautz,
Brown University; Robert G. Potter, Jr., Brown University; Enrico L.
Quarentelli, Ohio State University; Lee Rainwater, Harvard University;
Bernard C. Rosen, Cornell University; Alice S. Rossi, Johns Hopkins
University; Thomas J. Scheff, University of California, Santa Barbara;
Richard D. Schwartz, Northwestern University; Gilbert Shapiro, Boston
College; Eleanor B. Sheldon, Russell Sage Foundation; Edward Shils,
University of Chicago and Cambridge University; Herbert A. Simon,
Carnegie-Mellon University; Jerome H. Skolnick, University of Califor-
nia, San Diego; Pitirim Sorokin, Harvard University; Arthur Stinch-
combe, University of California, Berkeley; Norman W. Storer, Social
Science Research Council; Harrison White, Harvard University; Eu-
gene Wilkening, University of Wisconsin, Madison; Milton J. Yinger,
Oberlin College.

## SOCIOLOGY DEPARTMENTS PARTICIPATING
## IN THE QUESTIONNAIRE SURVEY

American University
University of Arizona
Boston University*
Brandeis University
Brigham Young University
Brown University
Bryn Mawr College
University of California, Berkeley
University of California, Davis
University of California, Los Angeles
University of California, Riverside
Case Western Reserve University
Catholic University of America
University of Chicago
City University of New York
University of Colorado*
Columbia University*
University of Connecticut
Cornell University
Duke University
Emory University
University of Florida
Florida State University
Fordham University
George Washington University
University of Georgia
Harvard University
University of Illinois
Indiana University
University of Iowa
Iowa State University
Johns Hopkins University*
University of Kansas
University of Kentucky
Louisiana State University

Loyola University
University of Maryland*
University of Massachusetts
University of Michigan
Michigan State University
University of Minnesota
Mississippi State University
University of Missouri at Columbia
University of Nebraska
New School for Social Research
New York University
State University of New York at
   Buffalo
University of North Carolina
North Carolina State University*
Northwestern University*
University of Notre Dame
Ohio State University*
University of Oregon
University of Pennsylvania
Pennsylvania State University
University of Pittsburgh
Princeton University
Purdue University
Rutgers, The State University
St. John's University*
St. Louis University
University of Southern California
Southern Illinois University*
Stanford University
Syracuse University
Temple University
University of Tennessee
University of Texas, Austin
Tufts University

* An asterisk indicates non-response to the questionnaire.

Tulane University
University of Utah
Utah State University
Vanderbilt University
University of Washington

Washington State University*
Washington University
Wayne State University
University of Wisconsin, Madison
Yale University

## RURAL SOCIOLOGY DEPARTMENTS PARTICIPATING IN THE QUESTIONNAIRE SURVEY

University of Connecticut
Cornell University*
University of Minnesota*
University of Missouri at Columbia
Pennsylvania State University*
South Dakota State University
University of Wisconsin, Madison

* An asterisk indicates non-response to the questionnaire.

# BIBLIOGRAPHICAL NOTE

The reader who wishes to extend his acquaintance with sociology might turn first to two general symposia. The first is *Sociology Today: Problems and Prospects*, edited by Robert K. Merton, Leonard Broom, and Leonard S. Cottrell, Jr. (New York: Basic Books, Inc., Publishers, 1959), which contains 25 essays by prominent sociologists on the different fields in the discipline. It was published under the auspices of the American Sociological Association. Another comprehensive introduction is *American Sociology: Perspectives, Problems, Methods*, edited by Talcott Parsons (New York: Basic Books, Inc., Publishers, 1968). Composed of about two dozen papers delivered originally as lectures in the *Forum* Series of the Voice of America, this book is intended more for the nonprofessional audience. Hundreds of special sociological topics are entered in the seventeen volumes of the new *International Encyclopedia of the Social Sciences* (New York: The Macmillan Company and The Free Press of Glencoe, Inc., 1968). Numerous introductory texts are also available. Two of the most widely used are Leonard Broom and Philip Selznick, *Sociology* (New York: Harper & Row, Publishers, 1968; fourth edition), and Alex Inkeles, *What Is Sociology? An Introduction to the Discipline and Profession* (Englewood Cliffs, N.J.: Prentice-Hall, Inc., 1964). Much of the scientific research conducted by sociologists appears in the general sociological journals, including the *American Sociological Review*, the *American Journal of Sociology*, and *Social Forces*, as well as the more specialized journals, such as *Social Problems, Sociology of Education,* the *Administrative Science Quarterly,* and the *Journal of Marriage and the Family.* Many of the problems of applied sociology are discussed in the pages of the large symposium, *The Uses of Sociology,* edited by Paul F. Lazarsfeld, William H. Sewell, and Harold L. Wilensky (New York: Basic Books, Inc., Publishers, 1967). This book was also published under the auspices of the American Sociological Association. In addition, two magazines—*Trans-action* and *The Public Interest*—often feature articles written by sociologists on social problems and public policy.